MUNISING SHIPWRECKS

Copyright 1983

ISBN O-932212-29-8
Library of Congress No. 83-70362

By Frederick
Marquette, Mich

A

F

GOING IN

Going In! Driven by roaring north winds, a schooner heads for certain destruction against the Pictured Rocks. Although not meant to depict a specific vessel, this sketch does accurately portray the general loss circumstances of the WABASH, GEORGE and ELMA.

Drawing by Edward Pusick

ACKNOWLEDGEMENTS

Producing a study of this nature by necessity requires a tremendous amount of assistance from a variety of people and institutions. It was only through their willing and professional help this compiliation was produced. I would like to thank the following:

Alger County Historical Society
C. Patrick Labadie, the Lake Superior Marine Museum
Tom Bathey of Venture North
Delta County Historical Society
Great Lakes Historical Society
Father Edward J. Dowling, S.J., an experts expert
Oscar and Kathy Froberg
Joe Geiss and Steve Lamphear of Three Little Devils
Mariam and Ewald Henke of Superior Outfitters
Jean Olson, for successfully deciphering my original manuscript
Mariners Museum, Newport News
Marquette County Historical Society
Marine Collection, Milwaukee Public Library
National Archives and Records Service
Peter White Public Library
Mrs. Janice L. Haas, the Rutherford B. Hayes Library
Eric Smith, a divers diver
Ken E. Thro, for his unselfish aid
George and Bettey Tomasi and their sons Rico and Vince for their able assistance.

FORWARD

Interest in shipwreck diving in Lake Superior has increased dramatically during the last ten years. This is especially true in the Munising bay area, where literally hundreds of divers from all over tne United States and Canada, spent their weekends exploring such interesting discoveries as the HERMAN H. HETTLER, the MANHATAN, the more recently discovered SUPERIOR, and probably the most exciting of all, the steamer, SMITH MOORE, which rests intact in the east channel in about 110 feet of water.

Frederick Stonehouse, a well known historian and author who has given us an insight into many of Lake Superior's shipwrecks in his books, **Went Missing, The Wreck of the Edmund Fitzgerald, Isle Royale Shipwrecks,** and **Lake Superior's "Shipwreck Coast",** and numerous articles, has now "brought to life" for both the historian and the scuba diver, the wrecks which have met their demise at Mother Nature's merciless whim in Munising's picturesque bay and surrounding waters. It affords the reader an opportunity to enjoy further the wrecks either by diving on them or simply taking a vicarious armchair trip down the anchor line.

Munising Shipwrecks will provide many hours of enjoyable reading and valuable historic information on an area now under consideration by the Michigan Department of Natural Resources as an underwater park preserve. It belongs in every avid diver's library.

Bettey Tomasi
Training Director
NMU Scuba School
Marquette, Michigan

TABLE OF CONTENTS

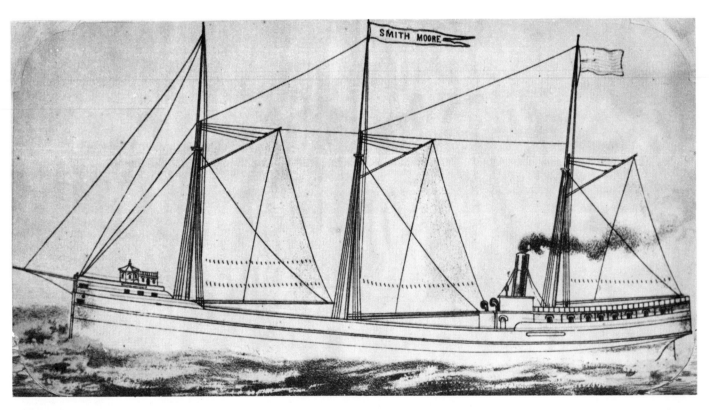

A lithograph of the most famous of the Munising shipwrecks, the steamer SMITH MOORE.   Authors Collection

Lake Superior Shipping; An Overview

Lake Superior played a very critical role in the development of the entire Upper Great Lakes region. Every major activity, fur trading, lumbering, or mining, used the lake as the highway to success.

The first commercial use of the lake was in the late 1600's by the early French voyageurs. Their goal was the region's rich furs. Initially the voyageurs used mere canoes until an increase in trade required the use of larger "Mackinaw" boats and bateaus.

Year after year, this hardy breed of intrepid men ventured north and west from the Soo, their destinations the scattered trading posts along the Superior shore. Principal posts were at La Pointe, Wisconsin, and Grand Portage, Minnesota. Minor posts were in the Pictured Rocks area at Grand Marais and Grand Island.

The first vessel constructed on Lake Superior was built in 1735 at Point Aux Pins, north of the Soo, for Louis Denis, Sieur de La Ronde. Only 25 tons, she was rigged with two sails. La Ronde used her extensively in the Apostle Island area and in various copper mining and fur trading activities.[1] The vessel made frequent trips from the Apostles to the Soo and it is likely she often passed or stopped in the Grand Island or Grand Marais areas.

Point Aux Pins saw another vessel, a 40-ton sloop launched some time after 1763.[2] The same area saw another sloop built in 1771, and in 1785 a schooner was hauled over the St. Marys Rapids.[3] The Lake Superior fleet was growing.

In 1763 the French lost the Lake Superior region to the English. Now it was the English traders that roamed the wild lake, and reaped the rich harvest of fur.

Vessel traffic on the lake hardly boomed. Before the War of 1812, there were only several small vessels above the St. Mary's Rapids. One was the 40-ton sloop FUR TRADER, later wrecked in an attempt to "shoot" the rapids while running down to the lower lakes. With the 1816 loss of the INVINCIBLE on Whitefish Point and the 1828 departure of the RECOVERY for the lower lakes, there were no vessels on the lake larger than a Mackinaw boat. This depressed state of navigation remained for seven years.[4]

The year 1835 saw the launching of one of the most famous vessels in Lake Superior history the schooner JOHN JACOB ASTOR, named for the owner of the powerful American Fur Company. Owned by the company, the 78-foot, 112-ton vessel was built of white oak from the Black River area of Ohio. The ASTOR, under the command of either of the legendary Stanard brothers, Benjamin or Charles, was used to carry passengers and freight between the scattered Lake Superior posts of the fur trading empire. In 1844 she was lost in a gale at Copper Harbor.[5]

After the ASTOR, the number of vessels on Lake Superior began to grow steadily. In 1837 another American Fur Company vessel, the MADELINE, was on the lake and engaged in fishing activities. The following year the 73-ton WILLIAM BREWSTER, 60-ton ALGONQOIN and 40-ton SISKOWIT, were all hauled over the St. Mary's Rapids into Lake Superior.[6] All were actively engaged in either trading or fishing.

The lake vessel count increased dramatically in 1845, with ten new vessels being hauled over the rapids. Unique among the fleet was the propeller INDEPENDENCE, the first steamer on the lake. This historic craft was lost in 1853 when her boilers exploded in the St. Mary's River. Other new vessels included the SWALLOW, CHIPPEWA, FLORENCE, UNCLE TOM, OCEAN, FUR TRADER (different from the earlier vessel), WHITE FISH, NAPOLEON, and MERCHANT.[7]

The sudden increase in shipping was caused by the twin discoveries of the vast iron deposits of the Marquette Range in 1840 and copper on the Keweenaw in 1844. Eagerly the new ships carried the men and supplies that would pioneer the new mines. Quickly the small settlements at Eagle Harbor, Eagle River, Marquette, L'Anse and Ontonagon assumed increasing importance as ports for the mining industry.

With the opening of the St. Mary's Fall Ship Canal (Soo Locks) in 1855, lake commerce boomed. Now ships could sail directly between Lake Superior and Lake Huron. Previously cargos had to be transshipped overland, an expensive proposition. If a vessel was to move from lake to lake, it was hauled out of the water and teams of oxen literally pulled it past the rapids on rollers. Over the years new, bigger locks were built as vessel traffic and the size of the ships increased.

Since the Soo Locks provided the means for cheap transportation of ore from the mines to the lower lakes mills, the iron mines stepped into high gear. Soon a veritable river of the red ore was flowing from the Ispheming and Negaunee shafts to the docks at Marquette. At first the ore was loaded into the schooners by the basketful. Later, when larger and stronger vessels were used, it was loaded directly into the holds by chutes. Unloading, however, was strictly pick and shovel work.

The ready availability of large amounts of iron ore, charcoal made from local hardwoods, and nearby deposits of limestone led many area businessmen to the conclusion that a major ironmaking industry could be established in the Lake Superior region. Between 1848 and 1922 thirty-three different iron forges or furnaces operated in the Upper Peninsula. The furnaces produced iron blooms or pigs that would be shipped to manufacturing points in Chicago, Milwaukee or Detroit. By night ships approaching the Marquette Harbor could see the deep red glow of the Marquette forge brightening the dark sky.

Two iron furnaces were in the Munising area. Near the present site of Christmas the Bay Furnace operated between 1870 and 1877. Today the site is a Forest Service campground. Part of the furnace is still standing and is a local tourist attraction.

The second furnace, the Schoolcraft or Munising Furnace, was within the boundaries of the Pictured Rocks National Lakeshore and operated from 1868 to 1877. Today little of the furnace is visible.[8]

Both furnaces required local shipping to bring in the supplies of raw ore and limestone, as well as carry out the cast iron pigs. The remains of pier structures can be found near each of the furnace sites.

The entire iron industry failed due to simple economics. It was far cheaper to transport large cargos of ore to the lower lakes and make iron there, than to make it locally. Also, a shift from charcoal iron to a coke based variety required the transport of large amounts of coke north to the Superior furnaces, an uneconomical proposition. Also, iron ore was a nearly indestructible cargo; rain heat, cold had no effect on it. Coke was far more sensitive and did not travel as well.

During the period following the 1855 opening of the Soo Canal, schooners were the predominant means of lake transportation, although the numbers of huffing, puffing, smoke belching steamboats were growing steadily. Abraham Williams, the earliest Grand Island pioneer, operated a fueling station for wood burning steamers for many years. Until coal supplanted wood as a fuel for steamers, the island was a popular stopping point to replenish cordwood stocks.

The high point for sail on the Great Lakes was 1868, when there were 1,856 vessels totaling some 294,000 tons. In 1873 the number had decreased to 1,663 vessels, but the replacement of older, smaller craft with newer, larger ones raised the tonnage total to 298,000! In comparison during the same year there were 2,642 hulls of all types on the lakes, totaling 521,000 tons. At the time, sail had 63 percent of the hulls and 57 percent of the tonnage! A well built and fast schooner was a good investment. With good management and a little luck, she could pay for herself in merely two years!

The decline of the graceful sailing vessel was rapid and steady. By 1880 there were only 1400 left on the lakes and by 1900 only 800! Many of those left had been converted to humble schooner-barges.

Sail craft declined for numerous reasons. They depended on favorable winds, and were difficult to maneuver in narrow and winding channels or rivers. Usually tugs were needed to pull them through these difficult stretches as well as in and out of harbors, all of which added to operating expense. As the lake traffic increased, the schooner cargo holds proved too small to be efficient.

Long since supplanted by the steamers in the passenger and general freight trade, the sailing vessels for a time found work hauling bulk cargos of iron ore, stone, coal and lumber. Gradually, however, these cargos also became uneconomical.

For a time many of the schooners found new roles as schooner-barges. These vessels were often nothing more than normal schooners with their topmast cut down and all sails and hamper removed except for the main, fore and aft. Since a small crew of four or five was carried, a schooner-barge could make some sail in an emergency, perhaps just enough to hold her head to the sea or haul off a rock coast if her towline parted.

"Strings" of up to six schooner-barges were towed behind a steamer or tug. This proved to be a very efficient arrangement, except for the large number of parted towlines which added constantly to the toll of wrecks.

The change from sail to steam also spelled the end of another kind of era, the time when a captain could own or be a part owner of his vessel and manage her affairs. The new steamers were too large an investment for a mere seaman. Instead the large shipping concerns owned and managed the vessels. The captain was reduced to nothing more than an employee. [9] No longer was he truly the master of his ship.

Along with the change of ownership came a change in names. Imaginative or graceful names like ANTELLOPE, ISLE ROYALE, LADY ELGIN, MOONLIGHT and SUNBEAM were gone. In their place the newer steamers were cursed with the names of corporate men. The JOHN B. TREVOR, CHESTER A. CONGDON, HENRY B. SMITH, and JOHN B. COWLE are prime examples. This insulting practive continues to the present day, with such incredible vessel monikers as STEWART J. CORT, WILLIAM R. ROESCH, and the nearly unbelievable S.T. CRAPO gracing the freighters of the inland seas.

New innovations were constantly occurring that revolutionized Great Lakes shipping. In 1869, the first bulk freighter, the 211-foot steamer R.J. HACKETT, was launched at Cleveland. With a capacity of 1,200 tons she was the prototype for an entire era of vessels.

In 1882 the first iron hulled steamer, the 287-foot ONOKO, was built. Although lost in 1915 in Lake Superior, it wasn't due to her iron construction but rather as a result of storm stress. 1886 saw the lauching of the first steel steamer, the 310-foot SPOKANE. In a short 17 years the quantum leap from wooden schooner to steel bulk freighter had been made.

Technology marched on. The nation's growing need of Lake Superior iron ore for the lower lake steel mills demanded still more efficient vessels. And the ship builders complied with longer, wider and deeper hulls.

In 1906, a mere eighteen years after the SPOKANE set the standard for new vessels, thirty-four freighters with a capacity to 12,000 tons and lengths to 550 feet were launched. The modern bulk freighters grew so rapidly that their capacity was nearly double those of only three years earlier. [10]

Along with the size, the cargo handling ability also increased. In the 1870's it took a week to unload 1,000 tons of ore with picks, shovels and wheel barrows. Now monstrous mechanical Hulett unloaders did the job in mere hours.

As a result of vessel size and subsequent economy, shipping rates also fell. In 1867 the rate for ore delivered from Marquette to Cleveland was $4.25 a ton. Five years later it was $2.50, and in 1897 a low $.50 per ton.

The cost to build new boats also fell, from roughly $7.00 a ton for a 2,500 ton vessel in 1885, to $5.00 a ton for a 5,000 ton vessel in 1898.

Traffic on Lake Superior grew as dramatically as vessel size. In 1889 only 25 percent of Great Lakes commerce was on Lake Superior. In 1906 she carried nearly half! More traffic in tonnage passed through the Soo Canal than the world famous Suez Canal.

In 1865 Michigan's Upper Peninsula mines were a significant producer of America's iron ore. By 1890 the Michigan mines were producing 45 percent of all the U.S. iron ore. At the turn of the century, the great Minnesota mines had also stepped into high gear. The Lake Superior iron district was supplying the vast majority of America's needs. Ship after ship heavily loaded with cargos of rich iron ore steamed down from Superior to the great steel mills of

Cleveland, Buffalo and Chicago.(By 1970 the figures had declined to a mere 15 percent, indicating a heavy reliance on cheaper foreign ores.) [11]

The number of shipwrecks increased directly in proportion to the amount of traffic on the lake. In the wake of every major storm, area newspapers would be filled with reports of numerous shipwrecks and missing vessels. The worst year for Superior was 1905, when 38 major wrecks were recorded. To date there have been approximately 550 major losses on Lake Superior.

In the twenty year period between 1878-1898, nearly 6,000 vessesl were wrecked on the Great Lakes. An estimated 1,090 were total losses. By contrast Lake Superior losses during the same period totaled approximately 137, with 80 being total losses.

Traditionally the navigation season on Lake Superior ran from the end of April to the middle of December. During the harsh winter the Soo Locks would close, effectively sealing off Lake Superior. As an examination of the vessel loss section will show, by far the most dangerous time for vessels was during the early spring and late fall. It was then that the lake could be expected to lash out with gales of incredible fury. Of the two periods, though, it was the fall that was the most vicious. Vessel after vessel succumbed to the "gales of November."

The area of Lake Superior running from Au Sable Point, Michigan west to Au Train, Michigan was an area of particular danger. The reasons are many and interrelated such that the total danger equals more than the sum of the individual parts.

The long coastline is irregular and presents a variety of features; high sand mountains at Grand Sable Dunes, towering rock cliffs of the Pictured Rocks, the long projection of Grand Island and the twisting sweeping shore near Au Train. All natural death traps of unwary vessels.

The prevailing north winds (which have an alarming propensity of turning into roaring north gales) could easily drive a vessel into destruction on any of the dangerous coastal features. Au Sable Reef, stretching north from Au Sable Point, is a hazard to be avoided at all costs. The entire coastline, but especially Au Sable Point, is notorious for thick fogs. Together all of these features spelled trouble for many vessels, and total loss for many others. Since a common navigational method was to "coast" along the shore, the special dangers described became obvious.

The appalling loss of life due to shipwreck on the east and west coast as well as on the Great Lakes eventually forced the government to construct lighthouses and other aids to navigation and to establish Life-Saving Stations in areas of high loss. The first government established lighthouse in America was built in 1716 at Little Brewster Island at the entrace to Boston. By 1789 a dozen lights were in operation on the east coast.

The first lighthouse on the Great Lakes was a beacon light at Ft. Nigara on Lake Ontario in 1813. By 1865 there were seven on Lake Ontario, twelve on Lake Huron, and twenty-six on Lake Michigan.

Lake Superior received its first light in 1849, although there is some confusion whether it was at Copper Harbor or on Whitefish Point since records indicate that both were established at the same time. Other Lake Superior lights quickly followed; Eagle Harbor in 1851, Raspberry Island in 1852, Marquette in 1855, Grand Island North in 1856, Keweenaw Bay in 1856, Gull Rock in 1867, Grand Island East Channel in 1869, and Au Sable Point in 1873. [12]

Through the years the number continued to increase until today there are 273 listed lights, beacons and official navigation aids on Lake Superior.

Two of the previously listed lights, the Au Sable Point light and Grand Island's North Light, are of particular interest to this book.

Au Sable Point, originally known as Big Sable Point, was a well-known danger to navigation. An early edition of the Mining Journal (Marquette) stated, "in any navigation of Lake Superior, there is none more dreaded (coastline) by the mariner than Whitefish Point to Grand Island." [13] Directly in the center of this coast was Au Sable Point and the dangerous Au Sable Reef. The Eleventh Lighthouse District was of the same opinion stating that the light "was more needed than any light in the district not already provided for." [14]

Construction on the light started in 1873 and on August 19, 1874 it was in operation. A French-made Fresnel lens made the light visible on the lake to a distance of eleven miles. In addition a hand-cranked fog horn helped warn ships off the deadly reef during a fog. Later a steam fired fog horn was installed. [15] Throughout the years numerous improvements in the form of a Keepers House, oil house, boat ways and sea wall were added. In 1910 the name of the light was officially changed from Big Sable Light to Au Sable Light by the Lighthouse Service.

Normal access to the station was by boat as no roads had been cut through the thick forest. Periodically a Lighthouse Tender would anchor offshore and use a small boat to land supplies on the beach or at the sea wall. On occasion small coastal steamers like the SOUTH SHORE also stopped to pick up mail or drop off supplies and visitors.

The nearest village, Grand Marais, was twelve miles to the east and accessible via a winding path along the beach at the base of the dunes. However, the waves of a rolling lake gale would quickly submerge the path, thus isolating the station. In the winter the only mobility was provided by snowshoes and dog teams. [16]

The weather at the isolated light was often terrible as judged by the descriptions entered by the keepers in their Lighthouse Journals. Keeper Beedon wrote on December 8, 1876, that the day started with a "light brees" from the south. By 5 p.m., "almost a hurricane (a) frightfull storm...it blew down 50 trees or more close by the light house and I thought that the (obliterated) light house and tower would blow down as they shook like a leafe the wind was N.H. West snowing and freesint it was the worst storm I ever saw on Lake Superior." [17]

Keeper Gus Gigandet noted in his entry for November 5, 1886, "one of the heaviest gales from the northwest with a blinding snowstorm, I have ever experienced for many years." [18] A following north gale rolled in on July 7, 1887, causing "the tower to shake hard." [19]

With the weather descriptions as fierce as these it isn't surprising to understand the toll of shipwrecks on the lake.

The men at the light fought the terrible isolation in a variety of ways. Some spent winters working in lumber camps, others hunted or fished. The Au Sable Reef was a popular and productive fishing spot.

The overriding method of relieving monotony was the tending of the light, polishing lens, trimming wicks, hauling oil, maintaining the building and grounds. The list was nearly endless, and it was certain that when the Lighthouse Inspector came, he would find deficiencies.

A good road didn't connect the light to the outside world until 1943. In 1958, in order to realize a reported $20,000 annual savings, the Coast Guard automated the light. Without the life in the lighthouse anymore, the light burned just a little bit dimmer. Although the Coast Guard still maintains the beacon, the lighthouse and grounds were transferred to the Pictured Rocks National Lakeshore in 1968.

Grand Island's North Light situated on a high bluff at the north tip of Grand Island, was orginally established in 1856. The present lighthouse was constructed in 1867. Like the Au Sable Light, the light is also presently automated, although the lighthouse is now a private dwelling. [20]

Munising's picturesque East Channel Light was built in 1867 to assist vessels in entering Munising Bay. In 1913 it was abandoned and the wooden structure has since deteriorated greatly. [21]

The Munising Range Front Lighthouse on West Munising Street and the Munising Range Rear Lighthouse at the end of Hemlock Street were built in 1909 to allow large vessels to enter the harbor. [22] Both are still in operation. The present Munising Coast Guard Station is Auxiliary manned.

An important service provided by the government was the establishment of Life-Saving Stations. The first such stations were on the east coast and manned strictly by volunteers, although the government did provide the equipment. After a series of disastrous shipwrecks it was evident that the system of volunteer stations would not work and a professional Life-Savings Service was formed.

The first United States Life-Saving Stations on Lake Superior were established in 1876 at Vermilion Point, Big Two Hearted River, Crisps Point, and Muskalonge Lake. These early stations were stations were thinly spread over the dangerous strip of shore known as the "shipwreck coast" running from the Whitefish Point west to Grand Marais.

Additional Life-Saving Stations were later built at Portage Ship Canal in 1884, Marquette in 1891, Duluth in 1896, Gand Marais, Michigan in 1900 (1899), and Eagle Harbor in 1911. Eventually stations were also opened at Grand Marais, Minnesota, Ashland-Bayfield, Wisconsin, and Whitefish Point, Michigan. [23]

In 1893 there were a total of forty-seven such stations in the Great Lakes, located in the areas of highest wreck probability. Each station was usually manned by a keeper and a minimum of eight surfmen, each numbered one through eight based on ability and experience. In the absence of the keeper, the number one surfman assumed charge. Although the crews were paid, they were only paid during the season. When the stations shut down in the winter, often only the keeper remained for a lonely winter vigil.

Quickly the rugged men of the United States Life-Saving Service built an incredible reputation for ability and courage. Time and time again these men performed the impossible, challenging monstrous seas and screaming winds to accomplish desperate rescues. Referred to as "storm warriors" in contemporary news accounts, their reputation was untarnished. They were the heros of the public.

In between the moments of incredible bravery, though, were long periods of monotonous inactivity and drill.

In 1915, under the impending threat of American involvement in a European war, the Life-Saving Service was combined with the Revenue Marine, Lighthouse Board and Steamboat Inspection Service into the present United States Coast Guard, thus ending a glorious chapter in American history. Although the traditions of the old Life-Saving Service continued for a short period in the fledgling Coast Guard, the eventual retirement of the original Life-Savers, increasing mechanization and a larger burden of official red tape slowly ended the legendary tradition of the "storm warriors." They now live only in history.

The Grand Marais Life-Saving Station, opened in 1900 (1899), was built on a site donated by the Grand Marais Lumber Company. [24] The rescue exploits performed by the Grand Marais Station crew were among the most spectacular in the Great Lakes. The Grand Marais Life-Saving Crew is long gone as the result of the change into the Coast Guard in 1915, but the facility is now manned by the Coast Guard and still in operation, performing a vital role in maritime safety.

The Munising Coast Guard Station, now the present Pictured Rocks National Lakeshore Headquarters, was opened in 1933. It was intended that the station would fill the large coverage gap beteen the Grand Marais Station and the Marquette Station. In retrospect, it was unfortunate the station wasn't opened 33 years before when it could have greatly contributed to the area's vessel safety instead of as late as it was. A Munising Life-Saving Station could have rendered valuable assistance in the 1895 loss of the ELMA, 1901 loss of the JOHN SMEATON and 1903 loss of the MANHATTEN among numerous other incidents.

The station crew only participated in two major rescues in its entire existence. The first was the SPARTA in November, 1940 described elsewhere. The second was the SINOLA near Fayette on Lake Michigan on November 12, 1940. The remainder of the station's efforts were directed toward small craft assistance.

The lack of activity at the station was directly the result of improved vessel safety. There just were not as many shipwrecks as in the hey day of the old Life-Saving Service. More important, they did not occur close inshore, within the range of the shore lifeboat stations. The old days of a brave Life-Saving crew battling their way through a thundering surf to rescue a ship's crew were long past. Now it was the large cutters and helicopters that made the headlines. The traditional spirit of the Life-Savers was dead.

In 1961 the station was officially abandoned and turned over to the City of Munising which later donated it to the National Park Service. [25]

As will be evident in the shipwreck listing, through the long history of Lake Superior navigation many vessels sought shelter from storms behind Grand Island or in Munising Harbor. This tradition still continues today.

On January 11, 1980 the 730-foot, 21,500-ton Canadian ore carrier ALGOBAY departed Marquette with a cargo of iron ore pellets bound for the Canadian Soo. In the open lake she was pounded by high waves and lashed by 55 mile an hour Northwest winds, causing her captain, Alexander Nazar, to seek protection in Munising's South Bay.

But, being unfamiliar with the channel, he first brought the vessel into shelter behind Grand Island, north of Trout Bay, on the east side of the Island. It was there that Joe Brey, a Munising fisherman, sighted the vessel at 5 p.m. Friday and inquired by radio if all was well. The Captain replied that as long as the wind was from the west, he thought he would be all right.

When Brey radioed the ALGOBAY again at 3 a.m. Saturday, the Captain said he was now worried since the swells were running at 15 feet and the wind had shifted more northernly. He was concerned the vessel could be forced aground. When Brey offered to guide the big vessel to safety in the harbor, the ALGOBAY's master agreed.

At daybreak Joe with his father Henry Brey and Gordon Synder used his small fishing boat to guide the ALGOBAY into the harbor where she safely weathered the storm. After the weather moderated on Sunday, she departed to continue her trip to the Soo. [26]

And so the long tradition of sheltering at Grand Island or Munising Bay continues. Today it was a modern ore carrier well equipped with radar, radio and depthfinder. Three hundred years ago it was a hardy French voyageur in a frail birch bark canoe. Regardless of the vast difference in technology, their purpose was the same!

There is another importanat facet to the ALGOBAY incident, namely that it very effectively illustrates the generous and efficient services rendered to those in need by the lakes commercial fisherman. When the men went out into the wild lake to guide the ALGOBAY to safety, there was no thought of reward, only that a vessel was in trouble and needed help. Without the assistance given by the commercial fishermen the large ALGOBAY could have been in serious trouble and the consequences fatal. The vessel was valued at $32 million dollars. Helping others has been a long tradition of the commercial fishermen.

It had been a saying of the old Life-Saving Service (and later the Coast Guard) that when a vessel was in trouble, no matter how wild the lake, you had to go out. Nothing, however was said about coming back! The commercial fishermen didn't have any dramatic sayings, nor did they share in the publicity given by the press to the colorful "storm warriors". But they did go out, regardless of the weather; the lake was their livelihood, nets needed to be set and lifted, the weather was only one more variable. They knew the lake as well as the hunter the forest, or the farmer his fields!

The commercial fisherman's rescue work was very important, especially in an area like Munising, too far from the Life-Saving Stations at Grand Marais and Marquette to be able to rely on their services. The short lived Munising Coast Guard Station was of little help. Although it isn't always documented in the following shipwreck accounts, in many instances it was the fisherman that actually rescued the helpless crews.

As it was in the past, so it still is now. Munising should be glad she still has an active commercial fishing fleet.

FOOTNOTES

1 Louise Phelps Kellogg, **The French Regime in Wisconsin and the Northwest** (New York: Cooper Square Publishers, 1968, pp. 352-355.

2 "First Trip by Steam to Lake Superior," **Michigan Pioneer and Historical Collections**, Vol. IV (1881), pp. 67-69.

3 James Davie Butler, "Early Shipping on Lake Superior," **Proceedings of State Historical Society of Wisconsin** (1894), p. 86.

4 Grace Lee Nute, **Lake Superior** (New York; Bobbs-Merrill, 1944), pp. 134-137.

5 J.B. Mansfield, **History of the Great Lakes**, Vol. 1 (Chicago: J.H. Beers, 1899), pp. 196-197.

6 Ibid., p. 196.

7 Ibid., p. 196.

8 Kenneth D. LaFayette, **Flaming Brands** (Marquette, Michigan: Northern Michigan University Press, 1977), p. 49.

9 Walter Havighurst, **Men and Iron** (New York: World Publishing, 1958), p. 88

10 Ibid., p. 95.

11 **Cliff News** (Cleveland: The Cleveland Cliffs Iron Co., Third Quarter, 1979).

12 **Light List, Volume IV, Great Lakes** (Washington, D.C.. U.S. Government Printing Office, 1979).

Charles K. Hyde, PhD, Director, The Upper Peninsula of Michigan, An Inventory of Historic Engineering and Industrial Sites. (Washington, D.C.: U.S. Government Printing Office, 1978), p. 140.

13 **Mining Journal** (Marquette), July 29, 1871.

14 Hyde, **Inventory**, pp. 124-125.

15 Hyde, **Inventory**, pp. 124-125.

16 James L. Carter, "Au Sable Light, Sentinel of the Great Sands," **Inland Seas**, Volume 33 (Summer, 1977), p. 100.

17 Carter, "Au Sable," p. 102.

18 Carter, "Au Sable," p. 102.

19 Carter, "Au Sable," p. 102.

20 Hyde, **Inventory**, p. 140.

21 Hyde, **Inventory**, p. 140.

22 Hyde, **Inventory**, pp. 158-160.

23 Julius F. Wolff, jr., "One Hundred Years of Rescues: The Coast Guard on Lake Superior," **Inland Seas**, Volume 31 (Winter, 1975), p. 256.

24 Dennis L. Noble and T. Michael O'Brien, **Sentinels of the Rocks** (Marquette, Michigan: Northern Michigan University Press, 1979), p. 27

25 Noble, **Sentinels**, p. 54.

26 **Daily Mining Journal** (Marquette), January 17, 1980.

The lonely and desolate coast near the Hurricane River.

Author Collection

The towering sand mountains of Grand Sable Dunes viewed east from Au Sable Point. Grand Marais is just arond the long sand point.
Author Collection

Au Sable Point looking west from Grand Sable Dunes. The light is the most westward finger of land.
Author Collection

Au Sable Light as viewed from the west. Grand Sable Dunes is clearly visible to the left.

Authors Collection

The 1895 Marquette crew was typical of the crew of the United States Life-Saving Service. The crew is seated in the heavy lifeboat. Keeper Cleary is at the tiller. The lighter surfboat is at the right.

Marquette County Historical Society

Marquette in the 1870's, a veritable boom town of Lake Superior commerce.

Marquette County Historical Society

Under full sail! A contemporary watercolor showing a topsail schooner of the MERCHANT's class about 1845.
Dossin Great Lakes Museum

An old engraving depicting a small schooner at the Soo Canal, approximately 1855. This type of small vessel was very common on the Great Lakes during the early days of navigation.

Canal Park Marine Museum

VESSEL:	MERCHANT
LOSS:	Total
DATE:	June 13, 1847
TYPE:	Schooner (brig)
LOCATION:	Grand Island

SYNOPSIS:

Research has so far indicated that the first major American vessel to join Superior's fleet of the "Went Missing" was the small 74-ton schooner MERCHANT. The schooner left Sault Ste. Marie on June 12, 1847 with a heavy cargo of mining supplies and foodstuffs consigned to the Keweenaw copper mines, seven passengers and a crew of seven.

Sources do not all agree regarding the number of crew and passengers. One source states she carried fifteen soldiers bound for Fort Wilkins on Keweenaw Point (Copper Harbor) as well as fifteen men employed by the National Mining Company. In my judgment the fourteen man figure is probably the most reliable.

Regardless of the crew size, the men were hardly over paid, at least by today's inflated standards. Average wages ran about one dollar a day!

Captain Robert Moore, her regular master, was not in command as on the day previous he had broken his leg while ashore. Instead, Captain Robert Brown of the schooner SWALLOW agreed to take the trip in his place.

Captain Brown appears to have been a sailor with a particularly irreverent twist of mind. On one occasion after hearing that Reverend John Pitezel, a famous Methodist missionary, had experienced an especially difficult storm-tossed trip on the brig JOHN JACOB ASTOR, Brown claimed the troubles were the direct result of having a boat full of women and preachers. He said he "never knew it to fail, with women and preachers aboard, sailors were sure to have storms"!

Pitezel couldn't understand why the "fair sex" (pre lib) would "influence the spirit of storms" against the sailors, unless it was in repayment for the many "long and painful neglects they have suffered from those who have followed the sea."

The MERCHANT left the Soo with an official destination of the Keweenaw area. Although as three of the passengers were Vermont lumbermen under contract to work at the L'Anse mills, the assumption can be made that a stop there was also planned.

On the night of June 13, a furious gale swept across Lake Superior, and presumably during this storm the MERCHANT sank. As news of the whereabouts of the schooner failed to reach the Soo, fears for the safety of the MERCHANT mounted. After three weeks, the conclusion that the vessel was lost, with all hands, was reluctantly drawn. To determine her fate, Captain Moore with another schooner searched the lake but failed to find a trace of the missing MERCHANT.

The only item of identifiable flotsam recovered from the lake was the schooner's companionway door, found on the north shore in the fall of that year by Captain Lamphere of the schooner WHITE FISH.

The case of the missing MERCHANT remained dormant for five years, until the summer of 1852 when a group of men coasting from Marquette to the Soo claimed to have sighted the topmasts of the schooner 30 feet below the water's surface in the vicinity of Grand Island. Although plans were made for the relocation and salvage of the wreck, they apparently, through examination of contemporary news sources, failed to bear fruit. Considerable excitement was generated when reports were circulated to the effect that among the lost passengers were agents of mining companies who had in their possession some $5,000 in specie. To this date no evidence has been found to indicate that the schooner was ever relocated, identified, or salvaged. So normally ends the story of the MERCHANT, just another vessel that was lost with all hands, in an unknown location in Lake Superior.

However, in this case if we leave the realm of historically verifiable evidence and enter the domain of speculation, some interesting possibilities come to light. Further, if we closely examine the evidence thus presented, we can draw some conclusions that might solve the mystery of the MERCHANT, and reveal her present location.

The original evidence that the schooner did leave the Soo for Portage of the date indicated is undoubtedly true. Contemporary newspaper accounts also agree that on the following day the lake was indeed swept by a fierce gale, a gale strong enough to have caused the small schooner to founder in the heavy seas.

We can surmise that the MERCHANT was probably overloaded, a not uncommon custom in the days prior to governmental regulations. Her overloaded condition would have made her easy prey for an unexpected gale. Evidence for the overloading is presented by Peter White, an early founder of Marquette. In later years White claimed to have sought passage on the fateful trip, but was denied as the schooner was already full. As room for an extra man was commonly made without comment, the schooner must have been full indeed.

As the passenger manifest included the three lumberman headed for L'Anse, the schooner undoubtedly planned a call at that port. The route from the Soo to L'Anse, whether of a direct nature or coasting along the south shore, would have carried the MERCHANT past Grand Island, at approximately the time the gale struck. The MERCHANT could have foundered outright, simply overwhelmed by the fury of the storm, or she could have elected to seek shelter behind Grand Island. Grand Island is the only shelter for 35 miles in either direction. The MERCHANT could well have foundered while enroute to shelter at Grand Island.

The evidence pointing to Grand Island as the location of the sinking is threefold. It was the area of the topmast sighting in 1852, Indian legend claims that a sailing vessel was seen there in a heavy squall at the time of the MERCHANT disappearance, and Grand Island would be about the right location for the MERCHANT to be at the time of the gale.

If the sighting by the coasting party was correct, we could assume that it was the remains of the MERCHANT they saw, as she was virtually the only sizable vessel lost in Superior to that time. However, the lake can play strange tricks on the eyes when peering down into its shadowy depths. These people may not have seen what they thought they saw!

The recovery of the companionway door on the north shore

can be entirely discounted as it was found too long after the sinking to be indicative of a possible location. The fact that no recognizable field of wreckage was ever reported located should not be considered overly important. At the time lake commerce was extremely light and communication poor. If such wreckage did exist, it might never have been located, and even if found, it might never have been recognized or reported. Further, a small schooner, heavily loaded, foundering quickly in a gale, would leave precious little evidence. It should also be remembered that no search was initiated until three weeks after the sinking!

After examining all available evidence, two conclusions can be drawn. First, that the MERCHANT's "disappearance" was caused by her overloaded condition coupled with an unexpected gale, and second, that her probable location is near Grand Island.

REFERENCES:

Archives. Bayliss Public Library, Sault Ste. Marie, Michigan.

"Autobiography of Captain John G. Parker," **Michigan Pioneer and Historical Collections**, Vol. 30, pp. 582-585, 1905.

Lake Superior News, July 10, August 14, October 30, 1847; September 8, 1852.

Mansfield, J.B. **History of the Great Lakes.** Cleveland: 1899.

Marquette Mining Journal, January 28, 1899; August 15, 1904.

Newton, Stanley. **The Story of Sault Ste. Marie**. Grand Rapids, Michigan: Black Letter Press, 1907. p. 151.

Pitezel, Reverend John H. **Lights and Shades of Missionary Life: Containing Travels, Sketches, Incidents and Missionary Efforts During Nine Years Spent in the Region of Lake Superior.** Cincinnati: Walden and Stowe, 1883. pp. 126-127.

Williams, Ralph D. **The Honorable Peter White**. Cleveland: Penton Publishing Company, 1907.

Wolff, Julius F. "They Sailed Away on Superior." **Inland Seas**, Winter, 1973.

VESSEL:	SUPERIOR
LOSS:	Total
DATE:	October 30, 1856
TYPE:	Sidewheeler
LOCATION:	Cascade, Pictured Rocks

SYNOPSIS:

One of the most spectacular and deadly of the Pictured Rocks shipwrecks was the tragic October 30, 1856 loss of the sidewheel steamer SUPERIOR.

The 567-ton SUPERIOR was built in 1845 in Perrysburg, Ohio. Together with the steamer SAM WARD she was hauled over the SOO Rapids for service in Lake Superior in 1854, a year before the famous canal opened. Under Captain Hiram J. Jones, she gained a reputation as a fine sea boat.

The best description of the events surrounding the wreck of the SUPERIOR is in the form of a letter from Joseph W. Dennis, one of the passengers, to the editor of the New York Daily Times. Although it is lengthy, the richness of its detail makes it well worth repeating in full.

"We left the Saut on the morning of Wednesday, the 29th October, weather being favorable until toward night, when it Commenced blowing from the northwest, raising a heavy sea. The boat rode very well until 11½ o'clock p.m., when she carried away her rudder, and immediately came round in the trough of the sea. The first sea that struck her afterwards carried away her smokepipes, throwing her freight and cattle down to leeward. The Captain and officers commenced throwing her deck-load overboard. This was found a difficult operation, on account of her being down almost on her beam ends, with heavy gangway planks lashed across her gangways, to keep the sea out. This had been done previous to her losing her rudder. It was now found that she was making water rapidly. Hands were called to man the pumps, but these were so small as to be of little avail. By 12 o'clock the water had entirely extinguished the fire in her furnaces, the engine stopped, and all hopes of saving her were given up. I then went from the deck to the cabin, to make preparations for going overboard, in case she should sink, as it was evident that she must soon do so. I divested myself of part of my clothing, in order not to be overladen. I then took two life-preservers, which had been thrown aside as useless, on account of the faucets having been rusted. These I tied round me under my coat, securing them by means of a sheet, which I tied over them. About this time the steward and the saloon-keeper began tearing off the doors of the cabin, laying them about so that they might be available for floats. I assisted them until the cabin was stripped on the windward side--the leeward being piled with furniture, stoves, etc. At this time the ladies were lying on the cabinfloor, calm and collected, and seemed waiting the event, whatever that event **might** be.

"At half-past one a cry was heard of 'rocks! rocks!' This brought all to their feet, and a rush was made for the boats, there being only two which could be got at; one on the promenade deck, just aft the starboard wheel--the other on the hurricane deck, right above it. The ladies were assisted into these boats by their friends. One young man from Superior City (Stephen Minter by name) had four sisters with him. When I last saw him he was sitting in the middle of a boat, and they were clingling to him in the vain hope that he might save them. Alas! they all found together a watery grave. At this time Capt. Jones came along and said, "You must not do anything rashly; stick by the boat, it is probable she will stand it when she strikes." They then threw over her small anchor, which held her until her stern struck the rocks. The first heavy sea broke her chain, and she came broadside on with a tremendous crash, which caused her to settle down very much.

"Previous to this, I had gone forward and got two stools, with tin cans under them--prepared for life-preservers. On my return through the cabin, I heard the Captain say to some of his crew, "this is the fourth boat I have lost, and it is probably the last." I lashed the stools together by means of a sheet, which I had brought from one of the staterooms--and as soon as she struck I jumped overboard, anticipating the time of her breaking up, as I saw she must very soon go to pieces. The first sea threw me nearly to the rocks, but its return carried me back. I turned around to look at the wreck, and saw that a heavy sea had carried away the cabin, boats and all, into the water, but the roar of the surf was so terrific as to prevent my hearing anything of the cries of the sufferers. The next sea came down upon me with a heavy load of timbers from the wreck, knocking me senseless and causing me to let go the stools. I sunk, and on coming to found myself strangling, and struggling to reach the surface, which I reached and caught two breaths, when another sea came on laden in the saw way. This struck me also, rendering me a second time senseless. When I recovered I found myself lying on my face on the rocks, with a heavy pile of driftwood upon me. Every sea that came in, however, brought its load, and at the same time lifted the whole mass, so that after a while I was able to extricate myself.

"Hearing voices beyond me, I crawled toward them, and found a number huddled together under the shelving rocks. The place where we cast was not earth, but was formed of fragments of rocks that had fallen from those that projected over. It was, I should judge, 100 feet long, by 5 broad. We shivered out the night, suffering intensely with the cold, and anxiously looking for daylight. All our efforts for fire proved unavailing. From the time the boat struck I am positive that she did not hold together more than fifteen minutes, before she was piled up on the rocks. At daylight we discovered that her wheels were left where she struck, about 200 feet from where we were, and projecting out of the water about 10 feet. On one wheel five persons were clinging--on the other two--still alive, every sea breaking entirely over them. They called to us for help, but it was of no avail; the sea running so high as to render it impossible, even had we the means within our reach.

"One by one we saw them, poor fellows, drop off, benumbed with cold, and unable to cling longer to this, their "forlorn hope." Among those whom we recognized on the wheels were the second mate, the steward, second clerk two saloon-keepers, and a fireman. The other we supposed to be a passenger. After passing a miserable day, we built a shanty, as best we could, of pieces of the wreck, wet mattresses, blankets, and pillows, and huddled into it, closely together for warmth.

"We were now eighteen in number. A young lad, of the name of Sisson, under the care of Mr. A. J. Foster, caused us much trouble during the night. Being deranged, he was roaming about, and it was with much difficulty that we could keep him down. On the morning of the second day we found the sea running still heavier than on the evening previous, and watched anxiously for it to subside, as our only chance of escape was by getting off in a boat. In the meantime we subsisted on some raw cabbage and some raisins. I left them and proceeded on alone, following in the trail of the men whom the mate had left. After traveling until 2 o'clock p.m. I began to feel extremely faint and weary, having eaten nothing since the night before. I found a few wintergreens which I ate, and some of the inside bark which I pealed from a fir-tree.

"The wind shifted about noon, and the sea run down almost immediately. We patched up one of the boats which came ashore, and managed to launch it. This was not an easy task, as we were wet, cold and hungry. Eight of our company got into the boat, the first mate, Mr. Davis, of Detroit, taking charge of her. We proceeded about two miles toward Grand Island, when four of us were landed, viz., the first engineer, one deck hand, one fireman, and myself, getting again very wet and cold, landing through the surf. My feet had now become so swollen, that I was obliged to cut open my boots from the toe to the instep. Mr. Davis left us and returned to the rocks, for the remainder of the party, promising to pick us up in the morning. This was about 4 p.m., and we wer to travel on during the night. We started into the woods in hopes of finding a house. We found the snow 16 inches deep, which caused intense pain to our chilled and swollen feet. We wandered through the night along the bank of the lake, finding only perpendicular rocks for some distance. In the morning we came to a small sandbeach, near the mouth of Grand Island harbor. Here we saw certain indications that the mate and his party had landed; also, that he had left part of his company and gone away with his boat. We learned, afterward, that he induced them to go ashore, and then left them privily, thinking, probably, that the boat was overladen. This party, so left, started through the woods, down the bay, hoping to find human habitation. Those who were with me, the engineer and his two men, finding that we were left, became disheartened, and said they would stay where they were till succor came, as the boat had taken with her all the provisions, consisting of some flour, some butter, and a few raisins.

"About noon, Saturday, Nov. 1, I overtook the men who had landed, they having got down off the rocks on to a point of sand, putting into the bay. We were now in sight of a house at the foot of the bay, the distance to which was about two miles across the water, and six or seven around by land, through a dense cedar swamp. These men had given up and laid down, intending to wait till some boat should come to their relief. I proposed going around the bay that night. To this proposition not one of them would accede at first. After shivering on the sand about two hours and getting a little rested, two of the number concluded to accompany me.

"We started at 2 o'clock p.m., walking on the beach and wading in the water. We reached the foot of the bay about dark. We had then, I should judge, about four miles to go, but the night was unusually dark and the tangled underbrush and fallen timber rendered the traveling extremely painful and difficult with our swollen feet and exhausted frames. My two companions soon fell behind, so that by 2 o'clock a.m., I heard nothing of them. I was at this time so much exhausted myself as to be unable to travel more than twenty minutes at a time. Then I would sit down and nap. This I scarcely dared to do, fearing that I should be unable to proceed, should I sit too long, or perhaps, that I should not awake at all.

"Painfully, indeed, was the remainder of my journey performed. Alone, far from home and beloved friends, in a bewildering forest, with my feet so swollen and benumbed as to be incapable of feeling, I felt almost at times about to give up. About an hour after daylight, however, I succeeded in reaching the house of Mr. Powell, who immediately took his boat and some provisions and went to look up the scattered suffering party whom I had left behind. He brought them all in, seven in number, in the course of an hour, and never did I behold such a wretched, wo-begone set of human beings. We rejoiced together over our almost miraculous deliverance, but soon the pain, caused by the warmth to our limbs, became almost intolerable. For three days, I suffered the most excruciating pain in my feet. They were black to my ancles, and these were so much swollen as to nearly fill up the legs of my pants. We were treated with the greatest kindness by Mr. Powell and his wife, their kindness seeming to me the more to be appreciated as provisions in those regions are **never** abundant. On the following Thursday the First Engineer, Mr. Coolahan, with four hands, started for Marquette, 40 miles distant, in order to intercept a boat to take us toward home. At Marquette, Capt. Ryder, of the propellor GEN. TAYLOR, heard the story, and came down and took us off. He also picked up the mate and his company, who had made their way to the lighthouse.

"We left Grand Island harbor on Sunday, the 9th, and landed at Detroit on Friday, the 14th Nov. On our arrival at Detroit we were kindly furnished--those who wished to go to Chicago--with passes over the Michigan Central, and myself with one over the Great Western Railroad. On arriving at Buffalo, my home, I called a physician, who pronounced my feet so badly mortified from exposure and chilling as to cause the loss of a part of my toes. This is probably owing to my having traveled one night longer than the rest of the men. I subsequently learned that the boy Sissons and a colored boy died after we had separated. The body of Capt. Jones was brought down to Detroit by the GEN. TAYLOR at the time we came down.

"Words are inadequate to express my joy and gratitude at arriving at my home, where I could procure medical aid, which I had for the past three weeks so much needed. Add to this the sympathy of kind relatives and friends. My physician tells me that I am doing as well as, under the circumstances, can be expected. I have the prospect of being laid up for the Winter, but this contrasts favorably with the one which we had at one time contemplated--that of being obliged to remain during that season near the scene of our terrible shipwreck, the horror of which will never, **never** be obliterated from my memory. The number of the lost, I should compute at about 42."

Joseph W. Dennis

On her last trip, the SUPERIOR departed from Chicago on October 25, with a cargo consisting of mining supplies. After clearing the Soo, her next stop was planned to be Marquette. When the news of her disaster reached the city nearly a week later, a public meeting was held and money and clothing collected for the survivors. A special relief party was sent to the wreck site. When it returned they reported everything was battered and torn to pieces against the rocks. The engine was later recovered for use in a sawmill. The loss of the SUPERIOR was placed at $25,000.

There has been a question regarding the number of lives lost. Dennis gave the number at forty-two, while the authoritative **History of the Great Lakes** states thirty-five lost and sixteen saved. **Merchant Steam Vessels of the United States** (The Lytle-Holdcamper List) lists thirty-four lost.

As is inevitable following a major loss, there were many accusations regarding the seaworthiness of the vessel. Some

authorities felt she was too old and rotten and never should have been permitted to carry passengers.

The site of the SUPERIOR wreck became a local tourist attraction of sorts, with numerous lake travellers stopping at the area to gawk. Local residents fished up small pieces of iron and other minor items from depths of twelve to fifteen feet. Today scuba divers periodically explore the wreck site although little of it remains due to ice and wave action.

REFERENCES:

Barbeau Papers, Bayliss Public Library, Sault Ste. Marie, Michigan.
Daily Mining Journal (Marquette). November 22, 1958.
Rawlson, A.L. "The Pictured Rocks of Lake Superior," **Harper's New Monthly Magazine**, May 1867.
Lake Superior Journal (Marquette), November 8, December 12, 1856.
Lytle, William M., and Holdcamper, Forrest R., eds. **Merchant Steam Vessels of the United States**. New York: The Steamship Historical Society of America, 1975. pp. 181, 228.
Mansfield, J.B. **History of the Great Lakes, Volume I.** Chicago: J.H. Beers, 1899. p. 677.
Marquette Mining Journal. January 28, 1899.
New York Daily Times. November 26, 1856.
Ward, Samuel. "Memoirs of Captain Samuel Ward." **Michigan Pioneer and Historical Collections**, Volume 21 (1892), pp. 336-367.
Wells, H., ed. "History of Accidents, Casualities, and Wrecks on Lake Superior" (manuscript compiled for the U.S. Army Corps of Engineers, Duluth, Minnesota, 1938), p. 3.

VESSEL:	LADY ELGIN
LOSS:	Recovered
DATE:	1858
TYPE:	Sidewheeler
LOCATION:	Au Sable Reef

SYNOPSIS:

The records are sparse regarding the incident but during 1858 the infamous LADY ELGIN briefly stranded on Au Sable Reef, receiving an estimated $1,400 in damages. The LADY ELGIN had stranded earlier in the season off Copper Harbor during a gale and sustained $8,000 in damages, a considerable amount for 1858!

The LADY ELGIN achieved its infamous status on September 8, 1860 when she perished on Lake Michigan with the loss of 283 lives. The LADY ELGIN was lost after a collision with the schooner AUGUSTA ten miles off Winetka, Illinois, about sixteen miles north of Chicago.

REFERENCES:

Lytle and Holdcamper. **Merchant Vessels.** p. 123.
Mansfield. **History of the Great Lakes.** pp. 683-684.
Wells List. op cit. p. 3.

The ill fated LADY ELGIN dockside in Chicago. Once briefly stranded on Au Sable Reef, in 1860 she would perish on Lake Michigan with the loss of 283 lives.

Author Collection

VESSEL:	Small Sailboat
LOSS:	Total
DATE:	June 2, 1859
TYPE:	Mackinaw Boat
LOCATION:	Off North Light, Grand Island

SYNOPSIS:

An especially tragic disaster occurred on June 2, 1859. On that date three youngsters from the Grand Island area, C.C. Williams, his sister Saphronia and their cousin William Clark, sailed to Marquette for a day of shopping. On the return trip they ran into a strong gale, and were forced far out into the lake. They were last sighted by the Keeper of the North Light, in the midst of high seas.

Later when the wind shifted and the storm abated, pieces of the boat drifted ashore, but the bodies were never recovered. Locally the accident became known as the "North Light Disaster."

REFERENCES:

Castle, Beatrice Hancom. **The Grand Island Story**. Marquette, Michigan: The John M. Longyear Research Library, 1974. pp. 61-63.

VESSEL:	ORIOLE
LOSS:	Total
DATE:	August 9, 1862
TYPE:	Schooner
LOCATION:	Grand Island

SYNOPSIS:

The ORIOLE, a 141-foot, 323-ton schooner under Captain Daniel McAdams, departed Marquette at 8 p.m. Friday,

August 8, 1862 with a cargo of 501 tons of iron ore bound for Erie. Aboard were nine crewmen, one passenger, the captain's wife, plus his mother-in-law, for an ominous total of thirteen.

The following morning at 7 a.m. the crack steamer ILLINOIS arrived in Marquette with her bow shattered from the keel to upper deck, and told of striking an unknown schooner in the fog off Grand Island Light! Reportedly when first sighted, the schooner was running directly towards the steamer and had she continued on course would have struck the ILLINOIS amidships. The ILLINOIS sheared off and as a result struck the schooner on her quarter.

Questioned by local marine men, the ILLINOIS passengers reported they had heard screams in the water following the collision and had supposed the schooner had gone down. They severely criticized the steamer's master, Captain Ryder, for not stopping to help the sinking schooner. They also stated the ILLINOIS was not blowing her fog whistle.

The mystery concerning the idenity of the schooner was solved Monday afternoon when the brig GLOBE under Captian J.H.Clifford came into port. Aboard was Andrew P. Fleming of Sodus, New York, the cook of the ORIOLE. The GLOBE had picked up Fleming drifting helplessly in the ORIOLE's yawl about six miles from shore 8 p.m. Sunday.

Interviewed in Marquette, the cook was in rough shape, with swollen limbs from forty hours exposure and lack of food. In spite of his injuries he told a damning tale of the disaster.

Fleming said he retired at a quarter past midnight on the 8th. At the time the schooner was running in fog, but it wasn't so thick that the signal lamps in the mast heads could not to be seen from deck. On watch was the Mate and three sailors. The four other sailors were asleep in the forcastle.

The schooner MOONLIGHT under full sail! In this photograph, with the square sail on the foremast, she is rigged as a barkentine. The MOONLIGHT was typical of the Great Lakes sailing vessels. The lost ORIOLE would have been much like her. A.F. Sagon-King Collection

The remainder of those aboard were in the aft cabin.

The steamer struck the ORIOLE on her starboard quarter, cutting directly into Fleming's cabin and literally slicing the schooner in two! When the stern separated as a solid piece, Fleming was thrown into the water. Hanging onto a piece of wood from the cabin, Fleming looked back and saw the remarkable sight of the schooner still under fullsail, but minus her stern! Seeing the steamer about fifty feet away he called for help, but received no answer. Looking back again towards the schooner, he saw it had disappeared into the gray gloom, as had the steamer when next he looked.

For a time he bobbed about in a sea of flotsam, which included several trunks and a half dozen women's dresses. All the while he could hear another voice out in the night. The unknown voice lasted for about an hour and a half, then all was silent.

Shortly after the wreck Fleming also heard the whistle of another steamer apparently following closely in the track of the first. Later he learned this was likely the SEABIRD,

known to be running behind the ILLINOIS.

About 8 a.m. he found the schooner's still floating stern. Crawling aboard he launched the yawl. But without oars, he drifted helplessly for forty hours until picked up by the GLOBE.

The Lake Superior News and Journal, the local Marquette newspaper, severly criticized Captain Ryder of the ILLINOIS' for not stopping and rescuing the ORIOLE survivors. The Captain, however, was defended by his clerk who stated that Ryder's first duty was to his vessel and to the safety of the 150 passengers aboard. One of the passengers was Mayor Duncan of Detroit.

According to the clerk, the captain's immediate action following the collision was to determine the extent of his own vessel's damges. After being lowered by rope over the bow to examine closely the damages, a sailor told the captain that they would fill in thirty minutes. Fearing for his passengers, Captain Ryder headed the ILLINOIS towards shore for about twenty minutes, until closer examination showed that he was in no danger of sinking and could safely make Marquette. The mate on watch at the time of the collision meanwhile told the captain that the schooner "appeared not much injured." To avoid any panic, the captain kept the knowledge of his damages from his passengers.

The clerk also said the fog wasn't consistent, but rather in banks. Just prior to the accident the ILLINOIS had left a clear area and thus they were not blowing a fog whistle. Regardless of the explanation, the local bitterness against the ILLINOS was unchecked.

Off Whitefish Point the propeller BACKUS recovered numerous items including the ORIOLE's wooden secretary containing her books and papers, a quantity of women's clothing, one gold watch, a lady's purse containing $48, some jewelry and several daguerreotypes of the captain, his wife and children.

Surprisingly, Captain McLeod of the schooner PLOVER discovered part of the schooner's wreck still floating eight miles north of the Pictured Rocks. Climbing aboard and examining the wreck, he reported the "hull was cut in two, with the bottom out and that the sides, masts, spars and part of the deck with sails and rigging were floating on the surface." The hat worn by the captain's wife when she was last in Marquette was the only trace of any person discovered aboard. Captain McLeod said the wreck was one of the saddest sights he had ever seen. He, like many others, was most critical of the performance of the officers of the ILLINOIS.

The schooner, with her cargo of 501 tons of Marquette Range iron ore, was a loss of $17,000.

REFERENCES:
Lake Superior News and Journal (Marquette). August 15, 22; September 5, 1862.
Portage Lake Mining Gazette. August 16, 23, 30; September 14, 1862.
Wells List op. cit., p.5.

The sidewheeler steamer ILLINOIS, the vessel that ran down the schooner ORIOLE and didn't bother to stop to pick up the survivors.

Marine Historical Collection
Milwaukee Public Library

VESSEL:	ONEIDA CHIEF
LOSS:	Total
DATE:	May 1868
TYPE:	Schooner
LOCATION:	Au Sable Point

SYNOPSIS:

The schooner ONEIDA CHIEF became a total loss on Au Sable Point after running ashore in heavy weather. She was carrying a cargo of pig iron from the Marquette furnaces.

REFERENCES:
National Archives, Microfilm T-729, **Marine Casualties on the Great Lakes, 1863-1873.** Record Group 26.
Wells List. op. cit. p. 9

VESSEL:	EVELINE BATES
LOSS:	Recovered
DATE:	Fall 1869
TYPE:	Schooner
LOCATION:	Bay Furnace

SYNOPSIS:
The EVELINE BATES was moored to the Bay Furnace dock

near the west entrance to Grand Island Harbor when a strong north squall blew her free and onto the beach south of the dock. The BATES had just arrived with a cargo of supplies for the Bay Furnace, most of which were still aboard her at the time of the accident. Since the schooner was in a sheltered spot, it was thought the BATES could be easily pulled off. In spite of the efforts of the Marquette based tug JAY C. MORSE, the BATES wasn't freed until the spring of 1870. She sustained damages of $1,800.

The BATES was built at Huron, Ohio in 1858. She was 233 tons, 128 feet by 26 feet by 10 feet. Owned by E.H. Dykes, her home port was Grand Haven, Michigan. She continued in service until 1896.

REFERENCES:
Mining Journal (Marquette). November 13, 25, 1869.
Marine Directory of the Great Lakes. R. Polk & Company, 1897.
Merchant Vessels of the United States, 1897.
Wells List, op. cit., p. 7.

VESSEL:	BURMUDA
LOSS:	Total
DATE:	October, 1870.
TYPE:	Schooner
LOCATION:	Grand Island

SYNOPSIS:

No record has yet been located giving the particulars of the loss of the BURMUDA, but sometime during October of 1870 the schooner was wrecked at Grand Island. Her master, Captain Tinney, visited her afterwards to salvage what was possible and reported she would be turned over to the underwriters and that no effort to raise her would be made. Since he used the term "raise" it can be suggested that she was sunk, as opposed to being "ashore" which usually meant being aground on inshore shallows.

The ultimate fate of the BURMUDA is clouded. Fourteen years later in October of 1884, there were reports of the tug KATE MOFFATT working on the wreck, now listed as being "ashore" at Grand Island. Whether the tug was simply recovering additional cargo and hardware, or working on actually raising the schooner isn't known. The results of their efforts are also unclear.

It is certainly possible that the BERMUDA was recovered following the 1870 wreck in spite of her captain's dire forecast. If so, she could have wrecked again in the Grand Island area prior or during 1884. Such problems of low value vessels often escaped official comment.

The BERMUDA had earlier wrecked during a gale on Shot Point, nine miles east of Marquette on November 19, 1869. Her loss was reported by her captain who hiked the beach into the city with the bad news. Aboard was a cargo of general merchandise which undoubtedly sustained heavy water damage. It was intended she would carry iron ore down.

Since she had four feet of water in her hold, was hard on the rocks and was suspected to have broken her back, she was thought to be a total loss. But during the following July, she was hauled off and towed to Detroit for repairs, which included replacing forty feet of her keel and a great deal of new bottom planking. The cost was $800.

The BERMUDA was built in Oswego, New York in 1869. Valued at $12,000 in 1880, she was rated at B-1 and registered at 394 tons.

REFERENCES:

Mining Journal (Marquette). November 20, 1869; July 23, October 29, 1870; October 4, 11, 1884.

VESSEL:	DREADNAUGHT
LOSS:	Recovered
DATE:	October 28, 1870
TYPE:	Schooner
LOCATION:	Grand Island

SYNOPSIS:

The schooner wreck in Murray Bay has long locally been called the DREADNAUGHT, although in fact it is the GRANADA (see page 24). Part of the confusion is undoubtedly caused by historical coincedence since the DREADNAUGHT did at one time go ashore in the general area.

One popular version of the DREADNAUGHT wreck has her leaving Marquette on November 13 (no year given). A short time later a northwest gale blew up and she disappeared into a snow squall. Nothing was heard of her until the following spring when she was reported sunk in Murray Bay. This version also tends to fit the reported circumstances of the GRANADA loss.

A more colorful tale has her springing a leak after departing Marquette and going to Grand Island Harbor to be beached for repairs. The captain put her firmly aground at the mouth of the Anna River and hiked to Wetmore to send for help. When he returned the next morning, he discovered the vessel had slipped back into the lake and the crew, asleep below, had drowned. The likelihood of this tale being true is somewhat lower than a bed bug's knee cap, but it is part of the legend of the fictional DREADNAUGHT. There is, of course, some confusion over how a vessel sunk off the Anna River moved to Murray Bay, but never mind.

In fact, the DREADNAUGHT did wreck **at one time** in the Munising area. On the morning of Friday, October 28, 1870, she went ashore near Grand Island Harbor. The DREADNAUGHT was downbound from Marquette with a cargo of ore, normally about 300 tons or so. Reportedly the schooner was in only seven feet of water and could be pulled off without trouble. The accident was reported by her captain when he returned to Marquette two days later to fetch the tug DUDLEY and a large steam pump. The tug JAY C. MORSE was also engaged to tow the freed schooner to the Soo.

According to local reports, the wreck could well have been caused by the captain's drunkeness. For two or three days prior to sailing, he was said to be intoxicated. Ominously, he was still "befuddled" when she finally left. When he returned for the tugs he was said to be only "partly sober," and after reporting the news of the wreck, he proceeded to celebrate in style. Only with great difficulty was he put aboard the DUDLEY for the trip to the wreck!

From the initial reports it can be surmised that the schooner was likely recovered, especially since a towing tug was already procured. Accidents as apparently suffered by the DREADNAUGHT were common, so she could have been pulled free without trouble or mention in the local press. However, damages were listed as $13,000, a rather large amount for an ore schooner.

REFERENCES:

Mining Journal (Marquette). September 24, October 1, 8, November 5, 1870.
Wells List. op. cit. p. 8.

VESSEL:	MARQUETTE
LOSS:	Total
DATE:	November 13-14, 1872
TYPE:	Schooner
LOCATION:	Mainland, west of Grand Island

SYNOPSIS:

The 131-foot, 400-ton, three-master schooner MAR-QUETTE was blown high and dry on the sand beach west of Grand Island by a strong north gale during November 13-14, 1872. Although salvage efforts were immediately made, they failed and the schooner was turned over to the underwriters. The following spring a special group from Detroit attempted to recover her, but discovered the winter storms and ice had destroyed the vessel.

Salvage efforts were not completely in vain, since all of the schooner's hardware was saved. Owned by E.B. Ward, her original cargo was iron ore. It can be suggested that she was headed for one of the local furnaces.

REFERENCES:

Marquette Mining Journal, November 23, 30, 1872; April 26, June 7, 1873.
Wells List. op. cit., p. 9.

VESSEL:	UNION
LOSS:	Total
DATE:	September 25, 1873
TYPE:	Propeller
LOCATION:	Au Sable Point

SYNOPSIS:

The UNION, a 434-ton propeller, was bound down from Marquette with a cargo of iron ore when an early fall gale forced her on the beach at Au Sable. Battered by the waves, she was a total loss of $30,000. A relatively new vessel, she was built in Manitowoc, Wisconsin in 1861 and was owned by Mark English of Green Bay.

REFERENCES:

Mining Journal (Marquette). October 4, 1873.
Lytle and Holdcamper. **Merchant Steam Vessels**. p. 218.
Wells List. op. cit., p. 10.

VESSEL:	T. MORRELL (F. MORRELL)
LOSS:	Total
DATE:	1874
TYPE:	Schooner
LOCATION:	Sand Point

SYNOPSIS:

The 144-foot, 369-ton schooner was downbound from Marquette with a cargo of ore when she was reported lost on a reef near Grand Island. The loss of the schooner and cargo was placed at $23,000. The following year the small steamer J.K. WHITE worked on the wreck, removing her gear and

part of the cargo. The schooner was apparently never recovered as what is believed to be her remains are located in shallow water on the Sand Point bar.

REFERENCES:

Mining Journal (Marquette). June 26, 1875, November 11, 1887.

VESSEL:	BAHAMA
LOSS:	Recovered
DATE:	October 10, 1875
TYPE:	Schooner
LOCATION:	Paul Point, Grand Island

SYNOPSIS:

The schooner BAHAMA was forced ashore on Paul Point, Grand Island in heavy weather. She was quickly pulled off by the steamer IRA CHAFFEE without great damage.

REFERENCES:

Marquette Mining Journal. October 16, 1875.

VESSEL:	CHENANGO
LOSS:	Total
DATE:	November 20, 1875
TYPE:	Schooner
LOCATION:	Wood Island Reef

SYNOPSIS:

One wreck that occurred as an indirect result of the pig iron industry in Onoto (Christmas) was the schooner-barge CHENANGO. She left Marquette with a cargo of iron in the mid-afternoon on the 20th in the tow of the tug JAY C. MORSE. By 6 p.m. both vessels were ensnarled in a thick snow squall accompanied by increasing seas. For reasons that are not clear, the tug cut free the schooner and ran into Grand Island Harbor alone. The CHENANGO attempted to run the west channel, but miscalculated and struck the reef near Wood Island.

The ten-man crew stayed on the schooner throughout the night, eventually being rescued in the morning. The schooner was a complete loss of $16,000.

The tug JAY C. MORSE also became a Lake Superior shipwreck. In 1889 she capsized and sank when she ran too close to the bank in the Portage Ship Canal in an attempt to avoid striking another steamer. The MORSE was apparently later recovered.

REFERENCES:

Cleveland Plain Dealer. August 5, 1889.
Marquette Mining Journal. November 27, 1875.
Wells List. op. cit., p. 11.

The tug JAY C. MORSE. After wrecking off Marquette in 1867, she was raised and returned to service, only to again wreck in 1889 in the Portage Lake Ship Canal. In between she was involved in several Munising area wrecks and recoveries. The above photograph was taken in Penquaming, Michigan, circa 1880. Note the large spread eagle above the pilothouse as well as the bell.

State Archives, Michigan Department of State.

VESSEL:	J.K. WHITE
LOSS:	Recovered
DATE:	Fall, 1877
TYPE:	Coastal Steamer
LOCATION:	Grand Island

VESSEL:	STARLIGHT
LOSS:	Total
DATE:	September 29, 1880
TYPE:	Sail Yacht
LOCATION:	Unknown (off Au Train)

SYNOPSIS:

According to local news accounts the small coastal steamer J.K. WHITE was brought to Marquette on November 11, 1878 by David Sang, a local hard-hat diver. The WHITE reportedly was ashore at Grand Island since the previous fall. The steamer was said to be in good condition in spite of having all of her machinery stolen while on the beach. Sang planned to equip the WHITE as either a passenger vessel or as a working tug.

REFERENCES:
Marquette Mining Journal. November 16, 1878.

SYNOPSIS:

The small STARLIGHT, employed to carry railroad supplies to the camps of the Detroit, Munising and Marquette Railroad, then under construction, departed Marquette on Tuesday, September 28. She successfully arrived at the camp at Sucker Bay, her first stop, and unloaded part of her cargo. According to later accounts in the local newspaper, the crew then proceeded to celebrate the success of their long voyage with the heavy use of intoxicants.

They must have spent some considerable time celebrating since when they finally departed a stiff northwester was blowing. Recognizing the danger, the railroad men urged them not to leave, but the fearless crew paid no heed.

Concerned when the STARLIGHT failed to reach Munising, a Mr. Hendrie, one of the railroad men, organized a search party. His efforts were successful as soon some pieces of the boat, including her sails and masts as well as several items from her cargo, were found on the beach near Au Train.

About three weeks later the body of the STARLIGHT's captain, Elmo Larmo, came ashore. Searching his pockets for positive identification, his pocket watch was discovered, which ominously had stopped at 7 p.m., the time it was surmised the STARLIGHT swamped in the seas. His was the only body of the five crewman aboard reported to be recovered.

REFERENCES:
Marquette Mining Journal. October 2, 9, 30, 1880.

VESSEL:	MARY MERRITT
LOSS:	Recovered
DATE:	September 7, 1881
TYPE:	Schooner
LOCATION:	Au Sable Point

SYNOPSIS:

The MARY MERRITT, a Canadian schooner with a cargo of square timber, was caught in a gale and blown on the beach about three miles west of Au Sable Point. All of the crew was saved. The schooner, however, was badly damaged and immediate steps to haul her off with the tug JIM HAYS failed.

Surprisingly the following year the tug WINSLOW pulled her off with little difficulty, and towed her to Detroit for a refit. The MERRITT was later sold and in the process had her name changed to DOT. As the DOT, in August of 1883 she sprang a leak off Grand Marais and sank.

REFERENCES:
Marquette Mining Journal. September 10, 1881; September 1, 1883.

VESSEL:	MARY JARECKI
LOSS:	Total
DATE:	July 4, 1883
TYPE:	Steam Barge
LOCATION:	Au Sable Point

SYNOPSIS:

The MARY JARECKI was another victim of the infamous Au Sable fog god. The 200-foot, 645-ton steam barge with an iron ore cargo was enroute from Marquette to the Soo when she drifted south of her intended course in the fog and ran hard on Au Sable Point at full steam. The force of the impact drove her nearly three feet out of the water at her bow.

Captain Everett, in an attempt to save his charge, immediately went to the Soo to secure the tug MYSTIC with a lighter and steam pump. The salvage efforts were useless. Try as they might, the water in the hull could not be lowered. Apparently the JARECKI was holed too badly.

In August the wrecking tug KATE WILLIAMS started to work on her. The tug spent several weeks in the effort, using divers to patch holes and even pontoons in an attempt to float her free. The wrecking captain was confident of success but the work was to no avail. The JARECKI remained fast. Eventually she went to pieces during the storm of September 24-25.

Built in Toledo in 1871, she was rebuilt in 1880. Rated A-2 by Lloyds of London, she was valued at $28,000. Insurance covered her for only $20,000. Including her cargo, she was a loss of $40,000.

REFERENCES:
Log of Au Sable Light Station, July 4 - September 25, 1883. National Archives, Record Group 26.
Marquette Mining Journal. July 14, August 25, 1883; July 4, 1884.
Wells List. op. cit., p. 14.

The 200 foot, 645 ton wooden steam barge MARY JARECKI wintering in the ice at Escanaba, Michigan circa 1875.
Delta County Historical Society

The MARY JARECKI in the ice with two schooner-barges. The barge at the left is unidentified, that on the right is the MR. WARNER. It is suspected this and the accompaning photograph were taken at the same time.

Canal Park Marine Museum

A section of hull timber on the beach west of Au Sable Point, thought to be from the MARY JARECKI.

Author Collection

A unique photograph of a four masted schooner in dry dock. She was typical of the many schooners that sailed the Great Lakes. The GRANADA in Murray Bay shows many of the same details visible in the photograph.

State Archives
Michigan Department of State

VEXILAR VIDEOSONAR®

Three sonar views of the schooner GRANADA in Murray Bay. Sonar can be a valuable tool in locating and evaluating shipwrecks. The straight line represents the surface, the wavy line the bottom.

courtesy Bruce Longman & the RIGHT HERE II

VESSEL:	GRANADA
LOSS:	Total
DATE:	1886 (circa)
TYPE:	Schooner
LOCATION:	Murray Bay, Grand Island

VESSEL:	WABASH
LOSS:	Total
DATE:	November 16, 1883
TYPE:	Schooner
LOCATION:	Pictured Rocks

SYNOPSIS:

Locally the wreck of the schooner in Murray Bay has been long known as DREADNAUGHT. Apparently this identification was erroneously given to the vessel as the result of a 1960 Marquette Mining Journal article concerning the salvage of part of the iron ore cargo for a rock and mineral show. In truth, however, the schooner is the GRANADA.

In a 1901 Mining Journal interview with a Captain McLeod of Buffalo, who was in town handling the salvage of another vessel, the ELIZA STRONG, the Murray Bay wreck was identified as the GRANADA. Captain McLeod stated that "she sank about fifteen years ago. She was laden with iron ore and bound down the lake when she sprung a leak and was run into the bay where she sank. Being loaded with iron ore it was unprofitable for the underwriters to raise her; she was left there to rot."

In June of 1960 local scuba divers extensively salvaged much of the ore cargo for souvenirs for a regional rock and mineral show. Today the schooner is rapidly deteriorating, having suffered greatly at the hands of marauding divers. Since the schooner is resting in a bare fifteen feet of water and usually buoyed, she presents a lucrative target. Every summer divers work actively to destroy her. Desperately, it seems, each diver tries to remove some part of her as a personal souvenir. They hack, pull, saw and grab in an incredible frenzy of vandalism. Soon the once proud GRANADA will be only a pile of rubble.

REFERENCES:
Daily Mining Journal (Marquette). June 11, 1960.
Mining Journal (Marquette). September 28, 1901.

SYNOPSIS:

The tug SAMSON was enroute to Marquette towing the coal laden schooner-barges WABASH, C.G. KING and C.H. JOHNSON when she hit heavy weather off the Pictured Rocks. During the height of the storm the tow cable to the WABASH broke. Soon the schooner-barge was driven on to the Pictured Rocks. The crew stayed aboard throughout the long, stormy night, suffering greatly from the drenching spray and freezing weather. The next morning they were all safely taken off.

During the storm the JOHNSON also lost her towline. Only skillful handling by her captain, William Parker, kept her from joining the WABASH. Before Parker could haul her off into the safety of the open lake, the schooner was driven to within 100 feet of the towering cliffs.

The WABASH, a casualty of $15,600, was fully insured, including her cargo of 680 tons of coal.

The same storm that ended the WABASH's days also spelled the end for the steamer MANISTEE. The MANISTEE had departed Ontonagon enroute for Portage (today Houghton-Hancock), never to arrive. A field of wreckage west of the Keweenaw provided the only clue to the loss of the steamer and the fate of the 23 people aboard.

REFERENCES:
Marquette Mining Journal. November 24, 1883.
Wells List. op. cit., p. 14.

The steamer MANISTEE. She was lost with all hands in the same storm that destroyed the WABASH.

Marine Historical Collection
Milwaukee Public Library

VESSEL:	E.A. MAYES
LOSS:	Total
DATE:	May 10, 1884
TYPE:	Schooner-barge
LOCATION:	Grand Island

SYNOPSIS:

During the fall of 1883 the tug MUSIC, towing the schooner-barges NELSON, FORSTER, RICHES and E.A. MAYES was steaming from Buffalo to Prince Arthur's Landing (today Thunder Bay). In the area of Au Sable Point, the small fleet ran into a heavy gale. To shelter from the rough weather, the tug brought her charges to Grand Island.

Since all of the barges were leaking badly and it was late in the season, the MUSIC left them in Trout Bay and returned with the crews to Bay City for the winter. Leaving barges to winter at Grand Island was not at all unusual. Normally the vessels would be grounded as close inshore as possible and anchored for safety.

The first week in May 1884, the MUSIC returned to continue the trip. After the crews rerigged the barges and pumped them out, the tug nudged them off their winter perches and reassembled its tow.

On Saturday, May 10, the MUSIC and her tows departed Grand Island. The lake was still filled with large floating chunks of ice and the vessels were constantly brushing into them. About seven miles out, a large piece of ice struck the MAYES forward, stoving in her old and rotten hull. Quickly the MAYES filled and sank bow first. She went down so fast her master, a Captain Bennett, and his eight man crew barely escaped. The barge and her cargo of 850 tons of stove coal were a total loss of $9,000. The MAYES was owned by Mitchell and Bartnell of Bay City.

REFERENCES:
Marquette Mining Journal. November 24, 1883; May 17, 1884.
Wells List. op. cit., p. 14.

VESSEL:	GLASGOW
LOSS:	Recovered
DATE:	August, 1884
TYPE:	Steam Barge
LOCATION:	Grand Island

SYNOPSIS:

The GLASGOW was upbound with a coal cargo for Duluth when a northwest squal forced her ashore at Grand Island. She had been trying to come in under the lee of the island's south point for shelter but took the island a bit too close. After jettisoning 75 tons of cargo and with the help of Captain Everett and the tug DUDLEY, the steamer was released.

REFERENCES:
Mining Journal (Marquette). August 16, 1884.

VESSEL:	SOPHIA MINCH
LOSS:	Recovered
DATE:	September 30, 1886
TYPE:	Schooner
LOCATION:	Grand Island

SYNOPSIS:

The SOPHIA MINCH, with Captain H.J. Trinter, left Ashland, Wisconsin Monday morning, September 27, in the tow of the steam barge A. EVERETT. That afternoon the steamer broke down while just behind the Apostle Islands. At 10 p.m. the disabled EVERETT found a tow to nearby Washburn, Wisconsin, and left the MINCH with instructions to proceed alone.

The schooner started with a good wind but just past the Keweenaw she struck a southwest gale accompanied by snowsqualls. Between Manitou Island and Stannard Rock she was forced to heave to. Later she attempted to run to Marquette for shelter but in the blinding snow was unable to find it!

The schooner bounded around in the wild lake without a clear idea of her position until Thursday when without warning the cliffs of Grand Island loomed before her. She attempted to change her course, but the old schooner began to pound too hard, so she altered her heading to try to sneak in behind Grand Island. But disaster struck and the schooner stranded on the sand spit at the southwest corner of the island.

The schooner, however, was resting easily and, sheltered from the seas, it was thought it would be easy to release. The captain made his way to Marquette where he arranged for tugs, which did recover the MINCH without trouble.

REFERENCES:
Marquette Mining Journal. October 2, 1886.

VESSEL:	REPUBLIC
LOSS:	Recovered
DATE:	November 26, 1886
TYPE:	Schooner-Barge
LOCATION:	Williams Island

SYNOPSIS:

A typical schooner-barge wreck occurred to the 139-foot REPUBLIC during the fall of 1886. On the morning of November 26, the tug NIAGARA left Marquette with a string of several schooner-barges downbound with ore.

Off Grand Island they ran into a normal rolling Superior gale that snapped the REPUBLIC's towline. In an attempt to seek shelter from the storm, Captain M.J. Galvin set what little sail he could and headed for the west channel and Grand Island Harbor. But the driving seas and powerful winds blew the small vessel into Williams Island. The crew safely escaped without injury.

Since the REPUBLIC was an old schooner having been built in 1854 in Clayton, Michigan, it was thought she was a total loss. Immediately her owners turned the vessel over to the underwriters.

In May of the following year, however, things looked much brighter. Captain Galvin returned and took another look at the REPUBLIC and thought she could be successfully hauled off. After a bit of effort she was and continued to sail.

REFERENCES:
Marquette Mining Journal. December 1, 2, 6, 1886; May 30, 1887.

VESSEL:	Sailboat
LOSS:	Total
DATE:	October 17, 1887
TYPE:	Large Sailboat
LOCATION:	Off Grand Island

SYNOPSIS:

Small craft were often the victims of Lake Superior's fury. One such vessel was a large sailboat owned by a Mr. Oudotte of Marquette. She left the city with a cargo of supplies intended for Johnsons' Mill near the Rock River. The sailboat was last sighted at 10 a.m. Tuesday by the Grand Island Light-Keeper. The boat appeared to be light, so the Keeper thought that it was on the return trip, but they apparently never arrived in Marquette.

REFERENCES:
Mining Journal (Marquette). October 22, 1887.

Photographed while ashore at Ashtabula, Ohio, the SOPHIA MINCH also went ashore at the southwest corner of Grand Island.

Dowling Collection

VESSEL:	RICHARD MOREWOOD
LOSS:	Total
DATE:	November 19, 1887
TYPE:	Schooner
LOCATION:	Grand Island (NW)

SYNOPSIS:

The RICHARD MOREWOOD was enroute to Port Arthur, Ontario, with a cargo of 2,500 barrels of oil when a northwest gale blew her off her north shore track and into the cliffs at the northwest corner of Grand Island. The schooner struck at 11:30 p.m. in the midst of a blinding snow squall. Laying broadside to the cliffs, she remained afloat until Monday when the seas subsided, allowing the crew of seven to escape to the island.

A Canadian vessel, registered from St. Catherines, the schooner was owned by her master, a Captain McPherson. The 268-ton MOREWOOD was built at Port Dover, Ontario by Waterbury in 1856 and rebuilt in 1874. The schooner, an $8,000 value, was only half insured, although the cargo, owned by Standard Oil, was fully insured.

Soon after the wreck, the tugs J.H. GILLETT and A.C. ADAMS, together with a scow, began to salvage the cargo.

The schooner RICHARD MOREWOOD photographed while a rotting hulk. Note the decrepit condition of the vessel as well as the hogged hull.

Dowling Collection

By June of 1888, nearly all of the cargo was recovered. Since the oil was "Canada Test," it could not be used in the United States so it was shipped to Winnipeg via rail.

Although the MOREWOOD was initially reported to be in a "bad place" and "her bottom full of holes," Marquette salvors eventually recovered her in July of 1889. Taken to Port Huron, she was rebuilt at a cost of $15,000 and renamed the E.B. PALMER.

REFERENCES:
Marquette Mining Journal. November 23, 28, December 1, 1887; June 30, July 12, 15, 1889.

The Canadian schooner KEEWATIN (next to dock). In this photograph she is still rigged as a full sailing schooner.
Dowling Collection

VESSEL:	KEEWATIN
LOSS:	Recovered
DATE:	October 20, 1888
TYPE:	Schooner
LOCATION:	William's Landing

SYNOPSIS:
The KEEWATIN, a Canadian schooner under the command of Captain John Keith, was downbound from the north shore with a cargo of block sandstone when she was mauled by a strong northerly gale. As the gale shifted from northeast to northwest, and back again to northeast, the heavily laden schooner was forced to alter her course each time. In the vicinity of Stannard Rock, the seas tore loose the schooner's yawl, thus stripping her of her only small boat.

On Saturday morning, October 20, while trying to enter Grand Island Harbor to shelter from the storm, the KEEWATIN struck a sand bar near William's Landing on Grand Island. Since they lost their yawl, the captain and crew were forced to remain aboard until Monday, when they were rescued by local men. Taken by train to Marquette, Captain Keith reported the accident.

Fired by the urgency of salvage the Marquette based tug F.W. GILLETT departed at 4 a.m. the following morning. By 8 a.m. she had completed the trip and was alongside the stranded schooner. Immediately she began to pump her out and to dredge out the sand around her hull. By 9 a.m. Wednesday the KEEWATIN was freed. Quick work had cheated the lake of another victim.

REFERENCES:
Mining Journal (Marquette). October 27, 1888.

VESSEL:	SMITH MOORE
LOSS:	Total
DATE:	July 13, 1889
TYPE:	Wooden Steam Barge
LOCATION:	East Channel

SYNOPSIS:
The most famous shipwreck in the Pictured Rocks area is that of the SMITH MOORE lost in the Munising East Channel on July 13, 1889 as the result of damages suffered in a collision. The 1,191-ton, 223-foot steamer was built by the Globe Iron Works in Cleveland in 1880 and owned by Harvey Brown of that city.

As in the ORIOLE disaster of 1862, the first news of an accident reached Marquette only when the other vessel involved, in this case the 223-foot steam barge JAMES PICKANDS, docked. When the PICKANDS arrived at 9 a.m. on the 14th, a number of deep abrasions could be seen plainly on her port bow. Some of the one-half-inch thick steel reinforcing plates were ripped open for nine feet!

Captain Ennis of the PICKANDS, on watch at the time of the accident, stated that at 4 a.m. on the 13th, he was approximately ten miles off Grand Island and running in a fog. Visibility was about 100 yards and his fog whistle was blowing. He heard a second horn, but the fog played tricks with the sound and he couldn't determine its direction. Suddenly the massive bow of another steamer came into view barely 75 yards ahead and slightly to port. The second vessel sighted him at the same time and signaled for a starboard crossing. Captain Ennis put his wheel hard over but still struck the other vessel, now recognized as the SMITH

MOORE, a glancing blow. Since the PICKANDS was light (without cargo), she bounced off. Ennis slowed and waited for a signal from the MOORE, but none came so he proceeded to Marquette, thinking the damage slight. He couldn't have been more wrong!

About 10 a.m., observers in Munising, including the keeper of the East Channel Light, witnessed a most unusual sequence of events. Two steamers appeared rounding Trout Point heading for the harbor. The lead vessel was towing the following one. About 300 feet shy of the sand spit that partially blocks the channel, the lead vessel cut loose the tow line. Five minutes later the second vessel sank. The curious Light-keeper as well as others rowed out and discovered the sunken vessel was the SMITH MOORE. Her masts were standing a full fifteen feet clear of the water and much of her upper works had broken off and were floating nearby.

The SMITH MOORE, under Captain Morrison, had departed Marquette at 2 a.m., July 13, bound for Cleveland with a cargo of 1,743 tons of iron ore.

Captain Morrison later stated he had sounded two whistles when he saw the PICKANDS and when she didn't alter course, blew two more. The PICKANDS struck him heavily, cutting deeply into his vessel. Immediately he knew it was only a matter of time before she sank.

Directly after the collision, the SMITH MOORE began blowing distress signals, but the PICKANDS never responded. When the fog cleared sometime later in the morning, the steamer M.M. DRAKE came to her assistance. She took off the sinking steamer's crew and after putting a line aboard, started the tow for Munising.

Several weeks following the wreck, the sunken SMITH MOORE was inspected by hard hat commercial divers in an attempt to determine if salvage was possible. Captain Dennis Sullivan, the Wrecking Master of the Milwaukee-based Commercial Union Insurance Company, visited her with

diver John Quin. After inspecting the wreck, Quin reported she was level in 90 feet and her hull was in good shape, but that her stern cabin and pilothouse were gone. Evidently they were blown off when she foundered. Her masts were still upright and judging from the green paint scrapes on one, had already been scrapped by a passing vessel.

Due to the nature of the cargo, soft ore which turns into a putty-like consistency when wet, therefore making it very difficult to work with, it was considered uneconomical to salvage her. The death sentence was passed on the SMITH MOORE.

As circumstance would have it, Captain Morrison and Captain Ennis did have an opportunity to discuss the unfortunate accident. Both captains met at the Soo Canal while downbound. Reportedly the dialogue was both vehement and "raw."

The SMITH MOORE was known as a fast steamer. In May of 1886 under a Captain White, she broke her own record from Marquette to Cleveland and return. From lighthouse to lighthouse she made the trip in five days, fifteen hours and ten minutes. The time included loading a cargo of 1,500 tons of ore. It was more normal, however, if she averaged seven trips in 60 days.

The SMITH MOORE was named for Captain Smith Moore. Captain Moore was earlier the master of the steam barge H.B. TUTTLE until July of 1880 when he resigned to take command of his "own" ship. How long Captain Moore remained in command of the MOORE is difficult to determine, but by July of 1886 he had changed vessels and was ironically the captain of the JAMES PICKANDS. The PICKANDS was also known as a fast ship.

Captain Moore was by any standard an enterprising man. He also owned the popular Marquette hotel, "The European House."

The SMITH MOORE's first visit to the Marquette docks

VEXILAR VIDEOSONAR®

Two sonar traces of the SMITH MOORE. The one on the left shows a cross sectional view while that on the right illustrates a view along her decks. Notice the bubbles from divers on the bow and stern. The sonar also shows how far off the bottom the steamer sits.

Courtesy Bruce Longman & the RIGHT HERE II

was in early September of 1880. Locally she was hailed as one of the finest barges in the trade and remained a popular vessel in the area. In July of 1881 she took a load of excursionists from Marquette on a day trip to view the famous Pictured Rocks.

The SMITH MOORE was nearly lost to fire in 1884. She was discharging an ore cargo in Sandusky when a fire broke out in the port. The steamer only escaped by wetting down and cutting away all smoldering rigging.

The PICKANDS later became a victim of Lake Superior shipwreck. On September 27, 1894, she ran off course in a smoke haze and struck Sawtooth Reef off the Keweenaw's Eagle River, becoming a total loss.

The SMITH MOORE was first publicly found by scuba divers in 1966. A group from Grand Rapids, together with a Detroit group, were reportedly seeking the steamer's mythical cargo of 350 barrels of whiskey and 150 barrels of silver ore. The vessel's actual cargo, of course, was iron ore and nothing more, but the truth has never deterred a treasure hunter!

According to reports, the divers stripped the vessel of many artifacts, including her bell and steam whistle. Another group later recovered one of her large wooden stocked anchors.

Today the wreck is a popular diving attraction being visited by hundreds of divers each year. Although nearly all of her small artifacts have been stolen by unscrupulous divers, the SMITH MOORE remains a very rare example of a type of vessel that for many years was vital to the trade of the Great Lakes. She is an important link to our maritime past.

REFERENCES:
Annual Report of the United States Life-Saving Service, 1895. Washington, D.C.: Government Printing Office, pp. 100, 306.
Cleveland Plain Dealer. July 14, 15, 17, 19, 20, August 5, 1889.
Daily Mining Journal (Marquette). August 26, 1966; October 21, 1967.
Marquette Mining Journal. September 8, 1883; July 4, September 6, December 13, 1884; May 9, 1885; May 29, July 10, 24, 1884.
Marquette Mining Journal. May 1, July 10, Sept. 18, 1880; June 30, 1881; Sept. 8, 1883; July 4, September 6, December 13, 1884; May 9, 1885; July 10, 24, 1886; July 15, 16, 19, 20, August 10, 1889.
Wells List. op. cit., pp. 18, 22.

VESSEL:	EMPIRE STATE
LOSS:	Recovered
DATE:	July 17, 1891
TYPE:	Propeller
LOCATION:	Au Sable Reef

SYNOPSIS:
On July 17, 1891 the passenger vessel EMPIRE STATE stranded on Au Sable Reef about one mile northwest of the lighthouse during a heavy fog. The following day, since the seas were blowing hard from the northwest and threatening the vessel, all 24 passengers and 10 of the crew came ashore to the lighthouse. Later in the day all the passengers were given passage on the propeller INDIA. The crew stayed at the lighthouse until the 19th waiting for the weather to moderate and allow them to return to their ship. On the 22nd the vessel was finally pulled free and continued on for the Soo.

REFERENCES:
Annual Report of the United States Life-Saving Service, 1892. Washington, D.C.: U.S. Government Printing Office, p. 184.
Log of the Au Sable Light Station, July 17-23, 1891. National Archives, Record Group 26.

VESSEL:	CRUISER
LOSS:	Total
DATE:	August 21, 1890
TYPE:	Small Yacht
LOCATION:	Chapel Rock

SYNOPSIS:
A small pleasure vessel that was swamped in heavy seas near Chapel Rock. Unfortunately, little additional information is available for what is certainly both an interesting and historically unique loss.

REFERENCES:
Wells List. op. cit., p. 19.

VESSEL:	GEORGE
LOSS:	Total
DATE:	October 24, 1893
TYPE:	Schooner
LOCATION:	Pictured Rocks

SYNOPSIS:
Another schooner lost at the Pictured Rocks was the 203-foot, 790-ton GEORGE. Under Captain C.C. Roberts, she was headed for Marquette with a cargo of 1,333 tons of coal consigned to the Pickands Company when she ran into storm trouble. At 6 p.m. on Monday the 23rd, the GEORGE left Whitefish Point under a fair south wind. By midnight she was past Au Sable Point Light and the wind began to shift and increase. When in sight of Grand Island North Light at 2:30 a.m. on the 24th, the wind veered to the northwest and in the words of Captain Roberts, ''began to blow great guns.''

The GEORGE altered course to run for the shelter of Grand Island. By 5 a.m. she was nearly in, when the gaff broke, then the foresail split! Minutes later the mizzen went to pieces. The GEORGE was left without enough sail to control her and was thrown to the mercy of the seas.

An hour and a half later the schooner was aground 100 feet off the rocks. Repeatedly she was struck with heavy seas. Since the towering cliffs prevented the crew from reaching shore directly, they lowered the yawl and rowed to safety at Grand Island.

An idealized drawing of the GEORGE rigged as a barquentine. It is hard to recognize the broken remains at the foot of the cliffs as once being part of this beautiful sailing vessel.

Courtesy Lake Superior Marine Museum

Roberts remembered that it "was a cold, wet, hard pull." The nine occupants were happy indeed when the island was reached. Local marine observers (and others) were pleased to notice that one of the schooner's crew was a buxom young Norwegian girl. (Unfortunately this was before the days of wet "T" shirt contests!).

The GEORGE was a broken wreck. The loss was cut somewhat when the tug C.E. BENHAM came down from Marquette towing the Marquette Life-Savers in their boat. Together they stripped the schooner of everything they could, an estimated $5,000 of gear. Owned by Miles Fox of Chicago, she was a loss of $28,250.

Today the bare ribs of what is thought to be the GEORGE can be found close inshore in approximately ten feet of water. On a clear day the outline of the wreck's remains is quite visible from the surface.

REFERENCES:
Annual Report of the United States Life-Saving Service, 1894. Washington, D.C.: U.S. Government Printing Office, pp. 109, 268.
Marquette Mining Journal. October 26, 28, 1893.

VESSEL:	ELMA
LOSS:	Total
DATE:	September 28, 1895
TYPE:	Schooner-Barge
LOCATION:	Miner's Castle

SYNOPSIS:

During the last days of September 1895, early fall gales lashed the Great Lakes unmercifully. Everywhere vessels and lake port residents sought what shelter they could.

In Manitowac, on the shore of Lake Michigan, the steamer WESTOVER barely made port with the schooner A.T. BLISS in tow, both badly damaged. The schooner had lost her entire deck load of lumber, as well as her entire mainmast and foremast.

On Lake Huron, the tugs RELIANCE, MOCKINGBIRD and AVERY struggled mightily with a massive log raft. Finally, after a desperate battle, they were able to bring it to shelter under East Tawas's Point Lookout.

Lake Ontario was also roiled by the gales. Two schooners lay disabled and helpless under the Buffalo breakwall. the
Continued on page 34.

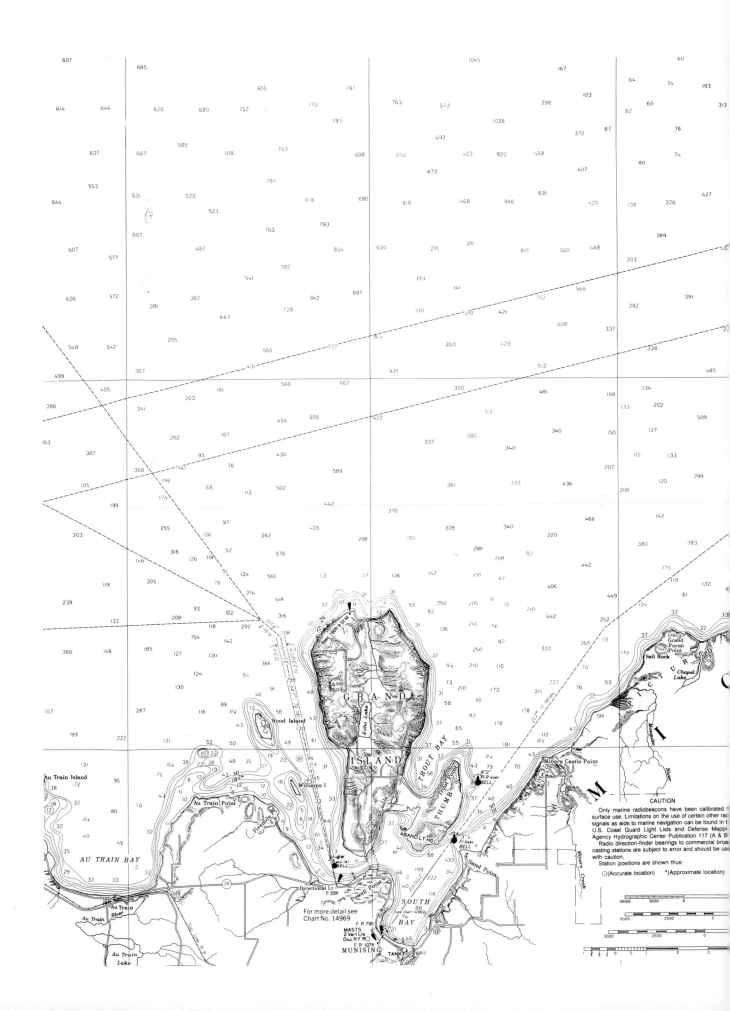

CAUTION

Only marine radiobeacons have been calibrated for surface use. Limitations on the use of certain other radio signals as aids to marine navigation can be found in the U.S. Coast Guard Light Lists and Defense Mapping Agency Hydrographic Center Publication 117 (A & B).

Radio direction-finder bearings to commercial broadcasting stations are subject to error and should be used with caution.

Station positions are shown thus:

⊙(Accurate location)   °(Approximate location)

For more detail see
Chart No. 14969

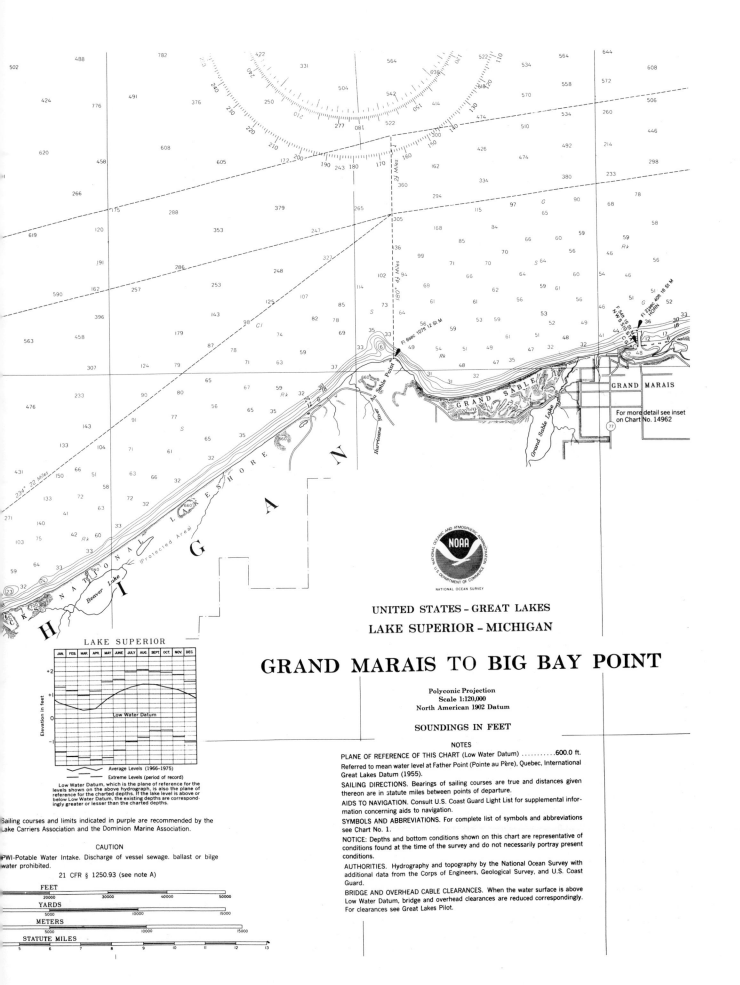

GRAND MARAIS TO BIG BAY POINT

UNITED STATES – GREAT LAKES

LAKE SUPERIOR – MICHIGAN

Polyconic Projection
Scale 1:120,000
North American 1902 Datum

SOUNDINGS IN FEET

GRAND MARAIS

For more detail see inset
on Chart No. 14962

LAKE SUPERIOR

Average Levels (1966–1975)
Extreme Levels (period of record)

Low Water Datum, which is the plane of reference for the
levels shown on the above hydrograph, is also the plane of
reference for the charted depths. If the lake level is above or
below Low Water Datum, the existing depths are correspondingly greater or lesser than the charted depths.

Sailing courses and limits indicated in purple are recommended by the
Lake Carriers Association and the Dominion Marine Association.

CAUTION

PWI-Potable Water Intake. Discharge of vessel sewage. ballast or bilge
water prohibited.

21 CFR § 1250.93 (see note A)

FEET
YARDS
METERS
STATUTE MILES

NOTES

PLANE OF REFERENCE OF THIS CHART (Low Water Datum) . . . . 600.0 ft.
Referred to mean water level at Father Point (Pointe au Père), Quebec, International
Great Lakes Datum (1955).

SAILING DIRECTIONS. Bearings of sailing courses are true and distances given
thereon are in statute miles between points of departure.

AIDS TO NAVIGATION. Consult U.S. Coast Guard Light List for supplemental information concerning aids to navigation.

SYMBOLS AND ABBREVIATIONS. For complete list of symbols and abbreviations
see Chart No. 1.

NOTICE: Depths and bottom conditions shown on this chart are representative of
conditions found at the time of the survey and do not necessarily portray present
conditions.

AUTHORITIES. Hydrography and topography by the National Ocean Survey with
additional data from the Corps of Engineers, Geological Survey, and U.S. Coast
Guard.

BRIDGE AND OVERHEAD CABLE CLEARANCES. When the water surface is above
Low Water Datum, bridge and overhead clearances are reduced correspondingly.
For clearances see Great Lakes Pilot.

The CHESTER B. Jones with a deck load of lumber. The lost ELMA was very similar.   K.E. Thro Collection

Continued from page 31.

business of the famous iron port was at a complete standstill.

At Port Colborne, another schooner arrived badly mauled by the gales. The PAUL struggled into the harbor with her bulkwarks, jib, mainsail and foresail carried away. Six miles from the breakwall, an unknown schooner was at anchor and flying distress signals. The severity of the storm prevented any attempt at rescue.

It seems, however, that vessels on Lake Superior were receiving the worst of the battering by the storm gods. Upbound for Marquette, the steamer CHARLES J. KERSHAW and her two tows, the schooner-barge MOONLIGHT and the KENT, were proceeding well, in spite of the rolling gale. With the lights of Marquette flickering in the distance, disaster struck. A critical steam pipe burst on the KERSHAW, completely disabling her engine. Without the steamer's power, all three vessels were at the mercy of the storm.

The MOONLIGHT and KENT were washed high up on a sand beach east of the city. Neither vessel was much damaged and both were eventually recovered, although the salvage effort required was long and expensive.

The KERSHAW was a different story. She was driven hard on the Chocolay Reef, several hundred yards offshore of the schooners. Her crew was rescued by the Marquette Life-Savers in one of the most spectacular operations ever conducted on the Great Lakes. In the KERSHAW rescue the Life-Savers truly earned their nickname of "Storm Warriors."

Storm conditions near the Pictured Rocks were just as fierce. The steamer WALLUDA, towing a whaleback barge, was mauled by the gale causing her to seek shelter behind Grand Island. The steamer had over five feet of water flooding her holds and her steam pumps could barely keep up.

The schooner-barge ELMA, together with the schooner-barges CHESTER B. JONES and COMMODORE, departed Baraga (Pequaming), Michigan under the tow of the steamer P.H. BIRCKHEAD on Wednesday, September 25. All carried large loads of fresh milled lumber consigned to lower lake markets.

Thursday the BIRCKHEAD and her "string" sheltered in Marquette from rough weather. When the lake calmed, sometime on Friday, the small fleet left to continue her long run down the lakes.

The calmer waters experienced on leaving Marquette were short-lived. As they made their way to the Soo, the lake grew rougher and rougher. By the time they reached Whitefish Point on Saturday, a full lake storm was blowing. Desperate for shelter, the steamer turned to run under Whitefish Point. Caught in the tenacious maw of the northwester, the towlines parted and the steamer lost her schooners.

The JONES was blown to within a mile and a half of the beach before her anchor caught, safely holding her off the breaking surf. Although surrounded by mountainous waves, the JONES held together throughout the gale. For two days, the local Life-Saving crew stood by on the beach in case the schooner began to drift ashore, making it necessary to try to rescue the crew. On Monday evening the 30th, it looked like the end had come for the schooner, so the Life-Savers launched their trusty surfboat and pulled the crew off. Even in somewhat moderated seas it was a difficult rescue. Several times the small surfboat capsized, but each time it was righted and the tough job continued. To the surprise of everyone, however, the JONES stayed together. Later the tug BOYNTON took the schooner and her crew through to Detroit.

After losing the tow from the steamer, the COMMODORE was able to set her shortened sail rig and ran for the safety of the Soo. Battered and leaking, she made it.

The BIRCKHEAD managed to pass a new towline to the ELMA and started to make for shelter at Grand Island. Near the Pictured Rocks, the towline broke again. The ELMA also broke her steering gear, preventing any attempt to use her sails as the COMMODORE did. Helpless, the schooner was blown before the gale, rolling so badly in the trough of the waves, she literally jumped her masts out! Without her deck cargo, long since washed off, and waterlogged, she was only a drifting hulk.

Unable to help, the BIRCKHEAD ran for shelter at Grand Island. Her captain hoped the schooner would wash up on the small sand beach near the Miner's River. It was the only stretch of good beach in the whole area that wasn't rock!

When the BIRCKHEAD reached Munising, her captain reported the accident and organized a rescue effort. Since the seas were too rough, he scouted the shore through the woods with George Prior, the Lighthouse Keeper. The only answer to their shouts was the crashing of the lake on the rocky shore. They would try again when the lake calmed, allowing

The same storm that wrecked the ELMA also wrecked the steamer CHARLES J. KERSHAW on Marquette's Chocolay Reef and threw her two schooner-barges, the HENRY A. KENT and MOONLIGHT on the beach east of town.

Marquette County Historical Society

Three of the principles of the ELMA wreck, the schooner-barges COMMODORE, and CHESTER B. JONES (in rear) and the steamer P.H. BIRKENHEAD.
Hamilton Collection
Rutherford B. Hayes Library

them to coast past the deadly cliffs.

To keep the ELMA afloat, the crew continuously pumped. Eventually the drifting hulk fetched up on a rock reef about 100 feet off Miner's Castle. The master, Captain Thurston, quickly dropped his anchors which swung the ELMA off the rock reef and eased her pounding. That night the chains parted and she was driven full on the rocks.

In an attempt to reach safety atop the towering cliffs, crewman George M. Johnson tried to row the ELMA's small yawl to the cliff base with a line. But the crashing waves splintered the fragile boat against the cliff. Johnson, however, managed to scramble up the cliff face until he reached safety, but lost the important line during the effort.

Rudolf Yack, another crewman, tied a line around his waist and attempted to swim ashore. He was dashed into the sharp rocks by the surf and killed. After numerous attempts, the crew stranded on the ELMA eventually succeeded in floating a line to Johnson. By the time this was accomplished it was too dark to try to bring the crew off. Throughout the long, cold storm-tossed night, the crew huddled on the ELMA, and Johnson huddled alone on the rocks, firmly holding the thin line.

With daylight, he made his end fast to a rock. One at a time, all of the crew safely reached shore, including the captain's three-year-old son and his wife. The youngster was hauled over the roiled water on a makeshift bosun's chair.

Using the line, the entire crew managed to climb to a small ledge about 75 feet above the lake. There they built a fire and waited until Tuesday morning when the storm moderated. With calmer seas, they started to build a raft for an attempt to reach the broken wreck for provisions. All they brought over on the line was a few loaves of bread and nothing more.

The ELMA's crew was finally rescued through the persistent efforts of the Light-house Keeper. At daybreak on Tuesday, he and a local fisherman started to coast the rocky shore looking for survivors or wreckage. A little after 8 a.m. they sighted the cold and hungry survivors.

Prior signaled the BIRCKHEAD which was three miles out

and on her way down to the Soo. The steamer happily returned and took the survivors aboard.

The ELMA was later examined by Captain Daniels of Marquette for the underwriters. He reported that as a result of the storm beating, her hull was broken and shattered, and she was rapidly going to pieces. Captain Daniels was, however, able to salvage a small amount of her lumber cargo.

In examining the wreck, Daniels saw the rope the crew used to climb the cliffs still dangling from the rocks. Daniels reported, "the man who went up there with that line must have been a good one, for he and some of his crew tried in vain to make the same climb."

Built in 1873, the ELMA was a loss of $9,000. Unfortunately she carried little insurance.

REFERENCES:
Annual Report of the United States Life-Saving Service, 1896. Washington, D.C.: Government Printing Office, pp. 88, 331.

Cleveland Plain Dealer. September 30, October 1,2, 1895.
Detroit Free Press. October 2, 1895.
Detroit Tribune. October 2, 1895.
Marquette Mining Journal. October 5, 17, 1895.

VESSEL:	NELSON
LOSS:	Recovered
DATE:	October 1, 1895
TYPE:	Schooner-Barge
LOCATION:	Powell Point

SYNOPSIS:

On the same day the crew of the ELMA was being rescued, a minor casualty occurred to the schooner-barge NELSON. The NELSON, together with the schooner-barge MARY B. MITCHELL, was under the tow of the steamer A. FOLSOM when they experienced trouble in entering Munising's west channel. The FOLSOM and her charges were just rounding the southwest point of Grand Island when the wind freshened causing the schooners to drift towards the beach. To prevent them from going aground, Captain Millard of the FOLSOM signaled for the schooners to drop their anchors until the wind lulled. The NELSON's crew was too slow, however, and she stranded in the shallow water on the west side of Powell Point, near the range lights. Although the NELSON was firmly aground in only five feet of water, water deep enough to float her was a bare fifty feet away.

Continued on page 38

A highly stylized rendering of the NELSON rigged as a barkentine before the days when she was cut down to a lowly schooner-barge.

Marine Historical Collection
Milwaukee Public Library

The NELSON wasn't in an exposed position and was easily recovered and towed to Marquette on October 17. After minor repairs to a damaged rudder, she loaded a cargo of ore and continued her career .

The NELSON was later lost in a tragic May 13, 1899 Lake Superior shipwreck. She was again together with the MITCHELL in the tow of the FOLSOM when they were struck by a freezing northwest gale west of Whitefish Point. In the heavy weather the NELSON's towline parted. Although the schooner was able to set enough sail to keep her head to the wind, she was badly beaten by the waves and her decks and rigging were covered by ice. When it was certain his vessel was lost, her captain placed his five-man crew and wife and daughter into the yawl. He then stayed aboard to swing out the davits.

When the boat was safely launched and secured to the schooner by a bowline, the captain jumped for the wildly bobbing yawl but missed and landed in the lake. Surfacing, he saw the schooner raise her stern high into the air and then plunge quickly to the bottom, dragging the yawl and its occupants down with it by the still attached line. Before his horrified eyes his wife and daughter, as well as his five-man crew, drowned! He survived and later floated ashore near Deer Park.

The NELSON was built in 1866. At the time of her loss she was valued at approximately $10,000.

REFERENCES:
Annual Report of the United States Life-Saving Service, 1900. Washington, D.C.: U.S. Government Printing Office. p. 179
Beeson's. op. cit., p. 139.
Cleveland Plain Dealer. October 2, 1895.
Journal of the Light-House at Whitefish Point. May 1899. National Archives. Record Group 26.
Journal of the Crisp Point Life-Saving Station. May 14-19, 1899. National Archives. Record Group 26.

Journal of the Muskallonge Lake Life-Saving Station. May 14-20, 1899. National Archives. Record Group 26.
Journal of the Vermilion Point Life-Saving Station. May 14, 1899. National Archives. Record Group 26.

VESSEL:	MICHAEL GROH
LOSS:	Total
DATE:	November 22, 1895
TYPE:	Steam Barge
LOCATION:	Pictured Rocks

SYNOPSIS:
The 142-foot, 290-ton MICHAEL GROH, under the command of Captain Michael Groh, was downbound from Marquette with a cargo of 325,000 feet of inch lumber when she broke a main steam pipe to her engine just east of Grand Island. Helpless, the prevailing northwinds blew her into the Pictured Rocks where she grounded on a rock reef just offshore, near the site where the ELMA had wrecked. Quickly she stove her hull in and sank up to her decks. The

crew took to her boats and escaped to safety ashore.

Rapid work by Captain John H. Gillett of Marquette, using the tug GILLETT and Captain Daniels with his schooner the CRISS GROVER, managed to save 140,000 feet of the cargo. However, the GROH was in a bad position and it was apparent that the first storm would destroy her. The feared storm arrived on November 30 and pounded the GROH to pieces, a loss of $9,000. Prior to that there was hope to pull the vessel free and the powerful Inman tug W.B. CASTLE had been telegraphed for from Duluth. The original lumber cargo, consigned to the Cleveland Sawmill and Lumber Company, was valued at $8,900. The schooner CRISS GROVER was a salvage veteran, having just returned from Isle Royale where she participated in the recovery of the wrecked steamer CENTURIAN and her cargo.

REFERENCES:
Mining Journal (Marquette). November 23, 30, December 7, 1895.
Wells List. op. cit.

VESSEL:	COMMODORE
LOSS:	Recovered
DATE:	November 14, 1900
TYPE:	Schooner-Barge
LOCATION:	Pictured Rocks

SYNOPSIS:
The storm gods of the lake are not only powerful, but also fickle, sometimes claiming vessels that seemed impervious to disaster and on other occasions sparing those that were ripe for the taking. One example of the lake's feminine behavior is illustrated by the trials of the schooner-barge COMMODORE.

The COMMODORE, in the tow of the steamer ELIZA H. STRONG, was bound for Portage Lake when the pair ran into a storm after passing Whitefish Point. Both vessels carried cargos of coal consigned to the Centennial Mining Company. During the stress of the storm, the towline parted and the COMMODORE was blown away from the steamer STRONG.

Battered badly by the waves and torn apart by the winds, the schooner was reduced to nothing more than a floating wreck. Her sails were gone, rudder carried away, and deck cargo of lumber swept off into the rolling seas. The crew decided their vessel was doomed! Launching their small yawl boat, the crew hurriedly abandoned the COMMODORE. Their exit was so fast, the captain left many valuables in his cabin. There was no doubt in the crew's mind that they would never see their vessel afloat again. If she didn't sink outright, she would surely be blown ashore or into the deadly cliffs of the Pictured Rocks. The crew was later picked up by the STRONG, who was searching for the missing COMMODORE.

To the crew's complete surprise, the next day the steamer located the COMMODORE still afloat, although certainly badly disabled. Since the storm had moderated considerably, the STRONG was able to take the COMMODORE in tow and bring her safely into Munising. The COMMODORE was left there for quick repairs while the STRONG continued on to Portage Lake. Eventually the tug J.W. WARD was to tow her either to Marquette or Houghton.

REFERENCES:
Daily Mining Journal (Marquette). November 16, 20, 1900.

VESSEL:	CHARLES H. BRADLEY, BRIGHTLE, MARY WOOLSON
LOSS:	Recovered all
DATE:	November 18, 1900
TYPE:	Wooden Steamer with two Schooner Barges
LOCATION:	Munising

SYNOPSIS:
Some shipwrecks occured not in fact, but only in people's imagination. A case in point is the "foundering" of two schooners on November 18, 1900.

At 11 a.m. on November 18, "Cap" Cleary, the Keeper of the Marquette Life-Saving Station, received a telephone message from Munising to the effect that two schooners were sunk in the channel between Grand Island and the mainland and the crews were desperately clinging to their rigging. Supposedly they were first sighted by a farmer who relayed the news to Munising.

Cleary immediately organized his crew and secured a special South Shore train for the run to Munising. Rapidly the well-drilled Life-Saving crew loaded the surfboat, cart and beach apparatus onto two flat cars. Since a coach was not available, the Life-Saving Crew simply took their normal seats in the surfboat and rode it as if they were riding the waves!

As luck would have it, their trip was not to be. Just as the train was leaving the rail yard, a message came through that the tug J.W. WARD had rescued the men from the schooners. After unloading their gear, the Life-Saving Crew returned to their station. It was the first time in the 1900 fall season they were called out.

Although the Grand Marais Life-Saving Crew was geographically closer, 32 miles compared to 37 miles in straight line distance, in terms of actual time required they were too distant to help. The Marquette crew could use the direct rail link provided by the South Shore Railroad and rapidly be on the scene. The Grand Marais Station was isolated and without a rapid transportation system.

Two days later the mystery of the two strange schooners was cleared up.

It seems that Captain Pecord of the tug WARD had discovered the steamer CHARLES H. BRADLEY, with the schooner-barges BRIGHTLE and MARY WOOLSON off Grand Island and had towed all three into a safe anchorage in Munising harbor. Apparently a small storm was blowing and the steamer had engine difficulties.

There never was a wreck, nor were the Life-Savers needed. The vessels were not in peril other than perhaps blowing ashore.

The tug WARD, together with the tug PETREL, had earlier departed Marquette for Munising with a large raft of cedar logs. Only luck placed her in Munising, and allowed her to earn a fat $300 towing fee for her owners.

The schooners were owned by O.W. Blodgett of West Bay City. Both were small vessels, the MARY WOOLSON built in 1888 while the BRIGHTLE was much older. The 804-ton BRADLEY, built in 1890, ended her days in 1931 at Portage Lake when she was destroyed by fire.

REFERENCES:
Daily Mining Journal (Marquette). November 17, 19, 20, 1900.

VESSEL:	ELIZA H. STRONG
LOSS:	Recovered
DATE:	August 31, 1901
TYPE:	Wooden Steamer
LOCATION:	Pictured Rocks

SYNOPSIS:
The same 205-foot, 781 ton steamer ELIZA H. STRONG that was involved in the COMMODORE incident in 1900 later became a storm casualty in the same area. The steamer was discovered badly damaged southeast of Stanard Rock by the steamer MUELLER and towed to Munising for repairs. The value of the steamer with her cargo of lumber was appraised at $10,000, giving an estimated salvage award of $3,000 to the MUELLER. After being towed into Munising the STRONG was allowed to settle in shallow water. The tug CHAMPION later raised her and she returned to service. The steamer had been bound for Buffalo when she ran into difficulties. The STRONG was built in 1899 and owned by the Strong Transportation Company of Tonawanda, New York.

REFERENCES:
Daily Mining Gazette (Portage Lake). September 21, 1901.
Daily Mining Journal (Marquette). September 25, 1901.
Duluth News-Tribune December 15, 1901.

VESSEL:	CONNELLY BROTHERS
LOSS:	Recovered
DATE:	November 12, 1901
TYPE:	Schooner-barge
LOCATION:	Sand Point

SYNOPSIS:
The small schooner CONNELLY BROTHERS dragged her anchors during a storm and was driven ashore at Sand Point. The steamer ZILLAH with the small tugs LAURA and HICKLER attempted to pull her free but were unsuccessful. When it was feared the schooner would go to pieces in the storm, the crew was removed by small boat. The following day the powerful tug SCHENCK arrived from Marquette and pulled the schooner free without damage.

REFERENCES:
Duluth News-Tribune. November 13-15, 1901.

The schooner-barge CONNELLY BROS. She stranded briefly on Sand Point.   Dowling Collection

VESSEL:	JOHN SMEATON
LOSS:	Recovered
DATE:	November 15, 1901
TYPE:	Steel Barge
LOCATION:	West of Au Train

SYNOPSIS:

The barge JOHN SMEATON, 458 feet long and 5,049 tons, broke her towline from the 461-foot steamer HARVARD during a north gale and was blown aground between Au Train Island and the mainland, about one and one half miles from the Rock River and five miles northwest of Au Train.

The SMEATON first struck bottom about one quarter mile out from shore, but the wind was so strong and the seas so high, the empty barge was literally bounced along the bottom until she finally grounded in six feet of water, a bare one hundred feet off the beach! Laying broadside to the beach, four of her eight compartments were flooded. She was listing badly and clearly hogged (center bulged up). Overall, the barge was certainly in bad shape!

The storm the SMEATON and HARVARD were caught by

was indeed fierce. All over Lake Superior vessels had sought shelter rather than brave the storm. Under Whitefish Point 19 steamers and 10 consorts (schooner-barges) were at safe anchor while at Marquette 21 steamers and 4 consorts waited for the northwester to blow itself out. Vessels caught in the open lake were badly hammered. The big steamer FRANK PEAVY had all of her deckhouse window smashed in and forward compartments flooded by the heavy seas.

At noon on the 15th of November, observers at Rock River, fearing the SMEATON was breaking up, sent for the Marquette Life-Saving Station crew. The South Shore Rail Road again assembled a special train for the Life-Savers, led by the legendary "Cap" Cleary. At 1:10 p.m., the special departed. Two flat cars were loaded with their surfboat and cart, while the crew rode in a single coach.

The use of special trains to transport Life-Saving crews was fairly common on the south shore of Lake Superior. In 1886 the Portage Lake Life-Saving crew used a special to go to Marquette to rescue the crews of the ROBERT WALLACE and DAVID WALLACE. A year later the crew made an identical run to save the crew of the schooner ALVA BRADLEY. To a large extent it was these 1886/87 wrecks and the long one-hundred-mile rail trips from Houghton to Marquette that persuaded a lethargic Congress to establish a Life-Saving Station at Marquette. The new station finally opened in 1891.

After a trip of less than an hour, the Marquette Life-Savers arrived at the Rock River. Loading their surfboat onto their cart, the eager crew headed down a rutted one and one half mile long wagon track to the beach opposite the wreck. The Life-Savers were preparing to lauch the surfboat when the SMEATON's crew signaled they were safe and did not desire to be taken off. Although the surf was still high and the vessel was continually being swept by the seas, her captain considered the crew in no danger. After holding the Life-Savers on the beach for several hours to give the barge's crew time to reconsider, Cleary brought his crew back to Marquette on the special.

Captain Joseph Kidd, a well known Great Lakes wrecker, representing the owners of the SMEATON, attempted to salvage the barge without success. His approach was somewhat basic. With the powerful wrecking tug FAVORITE and the smaller tugs SCHENCK and BOSCOBEL, he tried to simply pull her free. Kidd attached heavy hawsers from each tug to the barge and pulled away. In each instance, the tugs were stopped short with a terrific jolt when the hawsers grew taut! It was plain that a new method to free the barge was needed.

The legendary Great Lakes salvor Captain James Reid and his son Tom of Sarnia, Ontario were certain they had the answer. They were so sure of success they took the salvage contract on a "no cure, no pay" basis. If they did not succeed they wouldn't receive a dime for their efforts.

The Reids felt that by forcing compressed air into the barge's compartments it would force the water out, thus allowing the barge to "float" on a bubble of air. In such a state, a small tug could easily free her. The fact that this unique method had never been used on the Great Lakes before was of small concern to the Reids!

In actual practice the Reid's method worked almost as well as in theory. After caulking all cracks and leaks in the barge's decks and hull, air was forced into the compartments by two air pumps with a combined capacity of 800 cubic feet. Slowly the air forced the water out until the barge lost her list and came alive. The SMEATON was raised about two and one half feet until only her stern was still resting on the bottom. Gently the tug BOSCOBEL hauled the barge one thousand feet into deep water and later into safety at Marquette harbor.

When the barge arrived in Marquette on December 7 and was delivered to her owners, the Marquette Mining Journal hailed the Reid's success as the "greatest wrecking achievement in the Great Lakes."

It was fortunate the SMEATON was recovered when she was. Shortly after her safe arrival in Marquette, a strong norther' blew up that could have finished her had she still been on the rocks. Eventually she was towed by the steamer ROBERT L. FULTON to Superior, Wisconsin for repairs. Once in the drydock, a survey revealed over 160 plates (or roughly half of her bottom) had to be replaced at a cost of $50,000.

The Reid's fee was thought locally to be a third of the value of the barge, about $60,000. Other marine observers felt the fee was much higher, closer to $200,000. Either sum was an incredible amount for 1901, and for a mere three days of actual work!

Owned by the Pittsburg Steamship Company of the U.S. Steel Corporation, the SMEATON was valued at $200,000, and only two years old when wrecked. When the SMEATON was launched in Superior on June 17, 1899, over 15,000 people witnessed the event. A special train of 100 coaches carried spectators from as far west as Grafton, North Dakota, just for the occasion. The town fathers of Superior had decided to use the occasion to promote the advantages of Superior and the launching of the new barge was the catalyst.

REFERENCES:

Doner, Mary Frances. **The Salvager**. Minneapolis: Ross & Haines, Inc. 1958.
Duluth News-Tribune. November 16, 17, 18, 19, 27, December 1, 7, 18, 1901.
Mining Journal (Marquette). November 16, 23, 30, December 7, 1901.
Wright, Richard J. **Freshwater Whales, A History of the American Ship Building Company and its Predecessors**. Kent State University Press, 1971. pp. 146-147.

VESSEL:	CRESCENT CITY and Whaleback Barge No. 130
LOSS:	Recovered
DATE:	April 9, 1902
TYPE:	Steel Steamer, Barge
LOCATION:	Au Sable Reef

SYNOPSIS:

Both the 406-foot CRESENT CITY and the 292-foot barge were briefly on Au Sable Reef from April 9 through the 12th as a result of stranding in a fog. They were downbound from Marquette when a fog bank rolled in from the southwest, obscuring the dreaded Au Sable Point. Although the Lighhouse Keeper started firing up the steam-powered fog whistle at 6 a.m., when both vessels struck the reef at 6:15 a.m., enough pressure had not yet built up for it to start blowing.

To assist the stranded vessels the Lighthouse Keeper delivered a message to nearby Grand Marais calling for tugs and men to work shovelling the ore cargo overboard.

The Grand Marais Life-Savers soon arrived at the wreck site just in case their assistance was needed. Their lookout sighted the stranded vessels at 7:40 a.m. when the fog lifted enough to allow him to see the nine and a half miles distance to the reef. The Life-Savers were soon put to work shovelling overboard part of the iron ore cargo. Later they were joined by hired men from Grand Marais.

On the 10th, the tug GENERAL was on the scene but could not dislodge either the CRESCENT CITY or the barge. The next day another tug joined in and together they hauled the steamer free at 3 p.m. Finally at 9 a.m. the next day the barge was also freed. The barge had stove in one of her

The 406 foot steel steamer CRESCENT CITY shown on the rocks north of Duluth after in infamous November 1905 gale. Earlier, she fetched up on Au Sable Reef.

State Archives, Michigan Department of State

forward plates and only the still intact collision bulkhead kept her from flooding.

Since the barge was leaking badly, and a gale had started to howl, the CRESCENT CITY towed her to shelter at Grand Island for hasty repairs rather than try to continue the planned trip down the lakes. Because of the imminent possibility of the barge foundering, the Life-Savers accompanied them in their small surfboat towed astern of the barge. The forty mile trip lasted seven hours and was certainly a wet and cold one for the Life-Savers. Stranded by the gale at Grand Island they didn't get back to their station until midnight on the 14th. Luckily they hitched a tow back from the tug, GENERAL, saving themselves a very long, hard row.

The CRESCENT CITY later became a major wreck on Lake Superior on November 28, 1905 when she crashed against the cliffs north of Duluth during a terrible gale. She was eventually recovered at a cost of $100,000.

The barge was built at Superior, Wisconsin in 1893. Renamed the LYNN in 1911, she was scrapped in 1924.

REFERENCES:
Annual Report of the United States Life-Saving Service, 1903. Washington, D.C.: Government Printing Office, p. 145.
Log of Au Sable Light Station, April 9-12, 1902. National Archives, Record Group 26.
Wilterding, John H. **McDougall's Dream, the American Whaleback.** Duluth: Lakeside Publications, 1969. pp. 46-47.

VESSEL:	LIZZIE A. LAW
LOSS:	Recovered
DATE:	May 9, 1903
TYPE:	Schooner
LOCATION:	Au Sable Point

SYNOPSIS:

A basic problem faced by the old schooners was the very elemental one of leaking. Some of the older vessels developed an unholy appetite for water. It was not uncommon to have a large amount of water sloshing about in the hold, especially during heavy weather when seams were working. All of the water, of course, had to be pumped out by the crews, usually by using a steam pump. When a steam pump failed, it was a serious situation. Such a problem existed on the LIZZIE A. LAW on May 9, 1903.

The LAW was under tow when the line parted in a gale. Undaunted, the schooner made sail and ran before the sotrm. Unable to take the heavy punishment she was receiving, she anchored about three miles off shore and just to the west of Au Sable Point.

Sighting the distress signal made by the Au Sable Lightkeeper, the Grand Marais Life-Saving crew started out for the wreck. Their first try was in the surfboat under the tow of a tug, but the high seas forced them to return.

Undaunted, they next loaded the surfboat on a wagon, hitched up a team of horses and headed overland. They struggled about seven miles before the steep sand dunes forced them to stop. At this point they launched the surfboat and pulled for the schooner.

After a desperate row of nearly three hours, they reached the beleagured vessel. The LAW was indeed in rough shape. Her holds were filled with over seven feet of water, the sails were blown out and rigging sheathed in ice.

Removing the schooner's exhausted crew to safety at the lighthouse, the Life-Savers stood watch on the vessel throughout the long, wild night. At daylight they returned the crew to the vessel and set to work trying to save the vessel. After repairing the critical steam pump, the Life-Savers left for Grand Marais to secure a tug to tow her into port for more complete repairs. However, while they were gone, a passing steamer gave the LAW a tow to shelter at Grand Island. The schooner would live to sail again.

In October of 1908 the LAW did become a Lake Superior shipwreck, being wrecked on the east shore of the Keweenaw Peninsula during another Superior gale.

The LIZZIE A. LAW, built in 1875, was owned by the Hines Lumber Company of Chicago.

REFERENCES:

Annual Report of the United States Life-Saving Service, 1904. Washington, D.C.: U.S. Government Printing Office, pp. 157-158, 304-305.

Beeson, Harvey Childs. **Beeson's Inland Marine Directory.** Chicago: Harvey C. Beeson, 1908, p. 132.

Detroit Tribune. August 5, 1889.

Duluth News-Tribune. October 21, 22, 25, 1908.

The wooden steamer MANHATTEN (vessel on right) in the harbor at Conneaut, Ohio.   Dowling Collection

The MANHATTEN alongside an early ore loading facility. Note the open pilot station above the wooden pilothouse as well as the large search light.

Hamilton Collection
Rutherford B. Hayes Library

VESSEL:	MANHATTEN
LOSS:	Total
DATE:	October 26, 1903
TYPE:	Wooden Freighter
LOCATION:	Munising Bay East Channel

SYNOPSIS:

The Gilchrist steamer MANHATTEN, downbound from Duluth for Buffalo, was forced by north gales to shelter behind Grand Island. After the weather moderated late on the night of the 25th, the MANHATTEN started down the east channel for the open lake. About midnight, when she was opposite the Beacon Light, her steering chain broke, causing her to veer off course and strike a reef just off the channel.

No sooner had she struck, than a fire broke out. Apparently the force of the grounding knocked over a lantern which started the conflagration. It was the only explanation the captain and his mates could offer. When the fire could not be brought under control, the crew was taken off by the Powell and Mitchell tug WARD. The steamer burned to the water's edge, and together with her cargo of 76,000 bushels of wheat, was a total loss. The MANHATTEN was insured for $50,000 and the cargo for $65,000.

The 1,545-ton MANHATTEN, a comparatively modern and staunch vessel, was built in Detroit in 1887 and measured 252 feet by 38 feet by 19 feet. Owned by the J.C. Gilchrist Company of Cleveland, she was the **seventh** vessel of the Gilchrist fleet lost during the 1903 season. The others were the MOONLIGHT, WAVERLY, SWAIN, CRAIG, A.A. PARKER, and MARQUETTE. All were wooden vessels and oddly for the Gilchrist Company which made a frequent practice of saving money by not insuring their vessels, all were insured during the 1903 season.

Reportedly the burned out hulk later broke free of her rock perch and drifted to Sand Point. Salvors did recover some of her gear which helped to cut the loss. In 1920 the wreck was removed as a hazard. Today divers are exploring what is believed to be part of the steamer's hull timbers on the north edge of the east channel.

REFERENCES:
Annual Report, Lake Carriers Association, 1911.
Daily Mining Journal (Marquette). October 28, 29, 1903.
Duluth News-Tribune. October 28, 1903.
Wells List. op. cit., p. 32.

VESSEL:	SITKA
LOSS:	Total
DATE:	October 4, 1904
TYPE:	Steamer
LOCATION:	Au Sable Reef

SYNOPSIS:

Another victim of the treacherous Au Sable Reef was the 272-foot, 1,740-ton steamer SITKA. She was enroute from Marquette to Toledo with a cargo of iron ore when she wandered south of her course and at 6 p.m. on October 4, 1904, ran hard on Au Sable Reef. The SITKA found herself out two feet forward and on a rock ledge about a mile offshore with only twelve feet of water over it. The day of the accident was dark and misty, but there was no sea running or wind, thus the reason for the stranding isn't clear.

The Grand Marais Life-Saving Station first learned of the SITKA's plight at 7:30 p.m. from the coastal steamer HUNTER. The HUNTER was returning from Munising to Grand Marais and signaled the news of the wreck when she was abreast of the Station.

Rounding up his crew, Keeper Truedell launched his surfboat and pulled for the wreck, arriving about 11:20 p.m. after a three hour trip. The SITKA was discovered to be leaking badly but the crew wasn't ready to abandon her. The captain, however, asked Trudell to take several messages back to Grand Marais requesting tugs from the Soo to pull his vessel free. Instead of rowing back to port, Truedell landed one man at Au Sable Light and sent him back overland with the dispatches.

The Life-Savers remained on the beach at the Light-house and kept a close watch on the weather. At 5 a.m. on the next morning the wind and the sea had noticeable increased. Pulling out to the steamer, the Life-Savers found the crew was now ready to abandon her. Using the SITKA's two yawls and the surfboat, all seventeen of the crew plus all their baggage was safely landed on the sand beach at the foot of the Lighthouse.

The SITKA's crew then departed overland for Grand Marais, leaving their bags at the Lighthouse. The increasing seas and wind, however, weather bound the Life-Savers at the Light until 1 p.m. on the 6th. From the beach the Life-Savers observed that the gale and high seas broke the steamer in two. Interestingly, the storm-bound Life-Savers

The 272 foot, 1,740-ton wooden steamer SITKA, another victim of Au Sable Point Reef.   Dowling Collection

were furnished forty meals by Light Keeper Buffe at a charge of 25 cents each. Reimbursement was made through proper channels upon presentation of appropriate forms. Government red tape even existed 75 years ago.

On their way back to Grand Marais, the Life-Savers stopped at the wreck and salvaged her compasses and other valuable navigation instruments.

The following day, at the request of the master of the SITKA, F.G. Johnson and Captain Weeks, the Commodore of the Gilchrist Fleet, the crew in their surfboat was towed out to the wreck behind the tug SCHINECK and assisted in stripping her of salvageable items.

The SITKA was built in West Bay City in 1887, and owned by the Gilchrist Transportation Company of Cleveland. Although the SITKA was valued at $45,000 and the cargo at $8,225, making her a total loss of $53,225, no insurance was carried on the vessel. This was a common practice for the Gilchrist Company.

Today miscellaneous pieces of the SITKA litter the Au Sable Reef area. What is believed to be a part off her hull, measuring approximately 225 feet by 40 feet, can still be found in the surf line east of the Hurricane River.

Ironically, the HUNTER, the small coastal steamer that signaled the news of the SITKA's loss, was destroyed by fire the same day, while lying at the dock in Grand Marais.

REFERENCES:
Annual Report, U.S. Life-Saving Service, 1905. Washington, D.C.: U.S. Government Print Office, pp. 95, 296-297.
Beeson, Harvey Childs. Beeson's Inland Marine Directory Chicago; Harvey C. Beeson, 1905, p. 122
Duluth News-Tribune, October 5, 25, 1904.
Telegram, Grand Marais Life-Saving Station to Life-Saving Station, Washington, D.C., October 4, 1904, National Archives, Record Group 26.
Wreck Report, steamer SITKA, October 4, 1904, National Archives, Record Group 26.

VESSEL:	PORTAGE
LOSS:	Recovered
DATE:	1905
TYPE:	Wooden Steamer
LOCATION:	Au Sable Reef

SYNOPSIS:
The 1,608-ton steamer PORTAGE of Cleveland ran ashore near Au Sable Reef as the result of running off course. She was released after dumping approximately 500 tons of iron ore.

REFERENCES:
Carter, James L. Voyageurs' Harbor. Grand Marais, Michigan: Pilot Press, 1967. p. 66.

VESSEL:	MARITANA
LOSS:	Recovered
DATE:	September 18, 1905
TYPE:	Steel Steamer
LOCATION:	Grand Island

SYNOPSIS:
The steel steamer MARITANA, caught in a norther', sustained $15,000 in damages after scraping a Grand Island Reef.
REFERENCES:
Wells List. op cit., p. 35.

VESSEL:	ALTA
LOSS:	Total
DATE:	October 19, 1905
TYPE:	Schooner barge
LOCATION:	Grand Island

SYNOPSIS:
At 11 a.m. on Friday, October 20, the steamer MYER slowly worked her way out past the Marquette harbor breakwall. A heavy sea was still running from a two-day-old lake storm and the breakwall was being constantly inundated with rolling gray seas. The steamer had a decided list to port and her deck load of lumber showed the evidence of having been pulverized by the powerful waves.

The MYER had earlier attempted to shelter in Grand Island Harbor but when she reached the approaches a blinding blizzard totally obscured the channel. For safety her captain ran to Marquette.

Her captain also reported that she had lost two tows, the 178-foot schooner-barge OGLA and the 198-foot schooner-barge ALTA, during the height of the storm the past Thursday. All three vessels were downbound from Duluth with lumber for Tonowanda, New York, when they were caught by the storm off Grand Marais. The MYER attempted to reach shelter with his charges in Grand Marais harbor, but a 8 p.m. he lost both when their two lines snapped.

Both the ALTA and OGLA were at the mercy of the storm and were punished terribly. Together, they lost their deck loads of lumber as well as had their masts rolled out by the tremendous wave action. The ALTA also had her cabins swept off, while the OGLA lost her rudder.

Within two hours the ALTA was driven high on a Grand Island shoal. Her crew of six men and one woman (the cook, naturally) were rescued by small boats from Grand Island. All were reported utterly exhausted and had lost all their possessions in the wreck.

The OGLA was far more lucky. Her anchors caught just in the nick of time and her chains held her safely off the deadly Pictured Rocks. The beleagured and sorely tried crew stayed aboard until Saturday morning when they launched their yawl and reached safety.

The OGLA was later recovered and after repairs, returned to service. The ALTA, however, was a total loss. Even the famous wrecker Tom Reid, the hero of the SMEATON wreck four years before, couldn't save the old schooner-barge. Winter storms battered the ALTA into kindling.

The 935-ton ALTA was built in 1884 by Thomas F. Murphy at Cleveland, under sub-contract to the Wheeler yard.

REFERENCES:
Duluth New-Tribune. October 22, 30, November 22, 23, 1905.
Daily Mining Journal (Marquette). October 21, 23, 1905.
Wright. Freshwater Whales. op. cit., p. 116.

The whaleback barge SAGAMORE. She was similar to whaleback barge number 133.   Mariners Museum

VESSEL:	JAMES B. COLGATE
	Barge Number 133
LOSS:	Recovered
DATE:	September 21, 1907
TYPE:	Whaleback Steamer with Barge
LOCATION:	Grand Island

SYNOPSIS:

During a strong north gale the 308-foot whaleback steamer JAMES B. COLGATE with the 292-foot whaleback barge Number 133 were heading for shelter behind the bulk of Grand Island when trouble struck. The COLGATE wandered off course a bit and grounded, with the shallowed draft barge plowing into her stern. Although the damages were costly, both vessels were recovered with comparatively little effort.

The 1,713-ton COLGATE, built in West Superior, Wisconsin by the American Steel Barge Company in 1892, was owned by the Pittsburg Steamship Company at the time of her Grand Island grounding. The steamer was eventually lost due to shipwreck on Lake Erie on October 21, 1916. At the time she was owned by the Standard Transit Company of Minnesota.

Whaleback barge Number 133, 1,310 tons, built in West Superior by American Steel Barge in 1893, was also owned by the Pittsburg Steamship Company. Like the COLGATE, she also succumbed to loss by shipwreck, foundering in an Atlantic gale south of Fire Island, New York in 1911.

REFERENCES:

Daily Mining Journai (Marquette). September 22, 1907.
Wilterding. **McDougall's Dream**. pp. 36, 49-50.

The 198 foot schooner-barge ALTA. Note the donkey steam engine smoke stack abaft the forward mast. Intensive sonar searches have failed to locate any trace of the wreck.

Courtesy Lake Superior Marine Museum

The 263 foot, 1,748 ton CULLIGAN, formerly the George T. Hope. The twin stacks were a common feature of early steamers.

Courtesy Lake Superior Marine Museum

VESSEL:	ZENITH CITY
LOSS:	Recovered
DATE:	July 26, 1910
TYPE:	Steel Steamer
LOCATION:	Au Sable Reef

VESSEL:	CULLIGAN
LOSS:	Total
DATE:	September 27, 1912
TYPE:	Wooden Steamer
LOCATION:	Northwest of Grand Island

SYNOPSIS:

Another victim of the Au Sable fog was the 388-foot, 3,850-ton ZENITH CITY. Downbound from Marquette with iron ore, the large steel steamer plowed into the reef about one mile off shore. She was pulled off without trouble but received $10,000 in damages.

The ZENITH CITY was built in 1895 at the Chicago Shipbuilding Company for the American Steamship Company. When launched, she was one of the longest vessels on the Great Lakes. The ZENITH CITY was scrapped at Hamilton, Ontario in 1947.

REFERENCES:

Annual Report of the United States Life-Saving Service. Washington, D.C.: Government Printing Office, 1911. p. 128.

Van der Linden, Rev. Peter J., ed. **Great Lakes Ships We Remember**. Cleveland: Freshwater Press, 1979. P. 404.

SYNOPSIS:

Four hours after leaving Marquette with a cargo of 2,100 tons of iron ore, the 263-foot, 1,748-ton CULLIGAN was discovered to be leaking badly. Although she had leaked for several days, it was never serious and always within her pumps capability to handle easily. Now, however, there was no question that it had reached an alarming level. Accordingly her master, Captain Richardson, headed her for Grand Island where he intended to ground her on a shallow bar.

At 9:30 a.m. on the 27th, when it was apparent they were not going to make it, the captain and crew abandoned the CULLIGAN. With her boiler fires out due to the rising water, the steamer drifted until about 2:30 p.m. when she gave up the ghost and sank. As nearly inevitably occurs when a wooden steamer sounds, her pilothouse broke off and came bobbing to the surface. The crew was rescued by the fish tug COLUMBIA and taken back to Marquette. The CULLIGAN was a loss of $25,000.

REFERENCES:
Carus, Captain Edward. "100 Years of Disasters on the Great Lakes." Unpublished Manuscript, 1931.
Marquette Mining Journal. September 28, 30, 1912.
Wells List. op. cit., p. 48.

VESSEL:	SOUTH SHORE
LOSS:	Total
DATE:	November 24, 1912
TYPE:	Coastal Steamer
LOCATION:	7 miles west of Grand Marais

SYNOPSIS:

The small 73-ton, 84-foot SOUTH SHORE was steaming west from the Soo bound for Grand Marais on November 23 when she was engulfed in a strong northwest gale accompanied by blinding snow squalls. The storm, reputed to be the worst locally in fifteen years, broke up log booms in sheltered Munising Bay and toppled a pile driver off a scow and into the water. Since the huge seas prevented any attempt to enter the dangerous Grand Marais pierhead, the steamer's master elected to try to ride out the gale in the open lake.

Throughout the long wild night the small SOUTH SHORE battled the gale and in return was badly battered. By first light on the 24th the seams had opened and she was leaking badly. She had also lost part of her cabin as well as partially had her wheelhouse destroyed. Most important of all, the rising water in her hold had reached her boiler fires and extinguished them! Without power, she was helplessly driven before the gale. Desperately, the crew worked her hand pumps.

Shortly after 8 a.m., the Grand Marais Lifesavers lookout spotted the steamer about ten miles out. Although she wasn't flying distress signals, Captain Truedell, the legendary Keeper of the Grand Marais Station, bravely led his crew out into the storm-swept lake in their power lifeboat, nicknamed AUDACITY. When they reached the nearly awash steamer they attempted to save her by dumping cargo and working her pumps but when it became apparent that their efforts were futile, the Lifesavers took the four passengers and ten-man crew off. Later the abandoned steamer drifted to within 100 yards of the shore, eventually sinking in twelve feet of water.

Built in 1889, the SOUTH SHORE was a loss of about $8,000, although some small items to a value of $200 were later recovered from the wreck helped cut the loss. Owned by Emil Endress, she was captained by Ora Endress. The SOUTH SHORE was a frequent visitor to the Munising-Grand Marais area, hauling passengers and general freight up and fish down. Included in her stops were the string of Life-Saving Stations at Grand Marais, Vermilion, Crisp Point, Deer Park and Whitefish Point. Her loss was sorely felt.

REFERENCES:
Annual Report of the United States Life-Saving Service, 1912. Washington, D.C.: Government Printing Office, pp. 172, 99, 124.
Mining Journal (Marquette). November 26, 27, 29, Dec. 2, 1912.
Munising News. November 29, 1912.
Wells List. op. cit., p. 49.

The 73-ton, 84 foot coastal steamer SOUTH SHORE

Marquette County Historical Society

VESSEL:	HENRY B. SMITH
LOSS:	Total
DATE:	November 9, 1913
TYPE:	Steel Freighter
LOCATION:	Off Grand Island

SYNOPSIS:

The exact circumstances, as well as the location of the loss of the steamer HENRY B. SMITH are still, 67 years after the event, unknown. Since she sailed from Marquette, most locations are given relative to that port. However, directions could also be stated relative to Grand Island, especially since much wreckage came ashore in the general area. For these reasons, the story of the loss of the SMITH is included in a book on Munising shipwrecks.

By 1907 vessel size had increased dramatically. A new class of freighter known as 600 footers slid off the builders' ways with monotonous regularity. The capacity of the new freighters was huge. Just one of the 600 footers could carry a cargo equal to the combined capacity of every vessel on Lake Superior at the beginning of the Civil War! In 1895 the average ore cargo was 1,800 tons, by 1912 the average cargo was 7,740 tons!

The freighters owned by the big steamship lines made an average of 30 trips a season carrying iron ore down from Superior to the lower lakes, and returning in ballast. Those owned by the smaller concerns and independent shippers usually averaged only 20 trips, but carried well-paying cargos of coal up.

The key to success was speed; companies would tolerate no delays, either in loading or unloading their cargos, or in waiting for weather. These were fine new vessels; surely they had little to fear!

November has always been a bad month on the Great Lakes, but November of 1913 proved to be an exception. It wasn't just bad, it was catastrophic! Shipping disasters during the storm of November 7-11 accounted for the loss of 244 lives, with 17 vessels completely wrecked. Fifteen were steamers and represented a loss of over $7 million. Eleven were lost with all hands! Lake Superior saw the demise of six vessels: the steel freighter LEAFIELD, lost in an unknown location in the western end of the lake; the TURRET CHIEF wrecked east of Copper Harbor; the L.C. WALDO, blown on the rocks off Keweenaw Point; the barge ALLEGHENY, driven ashore west of Vermilion Point; the barge MARY McLACHLAN forced on the rocks off Port Arthur; and the steamer HENRY B. SMITH, lost somewhere in the lake. While the loss of any vessel is a cause for consternation, it was the disappearance of the SMITH that most disturbed the marine community.

Built in 1906, the 525-foot, virtually new, steel steamer was under the management of the Hawgoods of Cleveland. The 6,631-ton SMITH was valued at $338,000, insured for $325,000 and carried $30,000 worth of iron ore. Beeson's Marine Directory, the bible of Great Lakes shipping, considered her to be "one of the staunchest steel vessels on the Lakes." That she could be lost with all hands in a gale was totally inexplicable.

The SMITH's final voyage began at 6:30 p.m., November 9, when she cleared Marquette Harbor downbound for Cleveland. Deep in her holds she carried 9,500 tons of rich Marquette Range ore, a stable cargo for the rough seas she would be battling enroute to the Soo. The lake had been churned by northwest gales, but shortly after noon on Sunday, the wind dropped and the storm lulled. It was during this lull that the SMITH, with her crew of 25 men, departed.

Many people watched as the huge steamer plowed her way out into the still wild lake. One was Captain Fox of the steamer CHOCTAW, in Marquette with coal. Fox reported the SMITH "appeared to put about" after less than half an hour. Apparently the SMITH had found the going too rough and headed for the shelter of Keweenaw Point.

Sailors on the steamers DENMARK and CHOCTAW saw something else. As the SMITH was clearing port they observed her deckhands still battening the hatches! Since the SMITH had 32 hatches, each requiring individual attention, the process would have been lengthy.

Another observer was Keeper Cleary of the Marquette Life-Saving Station. Watching the SMITH weather the still mountainous seas, he expressed the opinion that Captain Owen would soon realize the folly of his ways and return to the safety of the harbor. Owen very likely did the former, but he never did the latter!

Shortly after the SMITH's departure, the lull ended and the storm attacked with renewed fury. The wind, which had been 31 mph when she left, quickly rose to 44 mph. These were land wind speeds. It was much stronger on the open lake. Some of the lucky vessels that survived the storm reported gusts in excess of 70 mph! This was the maelstrom the SMITH had confidently steamed into, with apparently unbattened hatches! With demonic power the great gale continued through Sunday night and into Monday.

Although the observers at Marquette had expressed fears for the safety of the SMITH, the marine community wasn't worried until Thursday, November 13, when she was overdue at the Soo. The owners wired inquiries to every port of the lake, but received only negative replies. The HENRY B. SMITH was missing!

Meanwhile, at Marquette, proof of an unidentified steamer's loss began to turn up on the beaches. First, it was in the form of wreckage coming ashore near the Presque Isle Dock. Consisting of oak paneling, parts of furniture and small pieces of lumber, it was definitely from a steamer, but was it from the SMITH? Keeper Cleary, after carefully examining it, concluded that at least part of it wasn't. Most likely the majority was from the steamer L.C. WALDO, wrecked on a reef off Manitou Island. But some portion of it could be from another steamer.

Earlier, when the steamer FRONTENAC docked on Wednesday, her master, Captain Murphy, reported one of his oilers had spotted a body floating in a lifebelt eleven miles southeast of the city, but rough seas made recovery impossible. If the oiler really did see a floater, who was to be sure it was from the SMITH?

On Thursday the 14th, Dan Johnson, a local landlooker, came into Marquette bearing an oar marked "HENRY B. SMITH". Johnson said he found it, plus three other oars and

The 525 foot steamer HENRY B. SMITH later in her career.   The Mariners Museum

a marked pike pole, on the beach east of Marquette, between Chocolay and Shot Point. Littered along the water's edge east of Chocolay were also small bits of wreckage, evidently from the upper works of a steamer. Further on, near Shot Point, the beaches were filled with a considerable amount of wreckage. Among it were pieces of a white deck house. White was the color of the SMITH's deck house.

Johnson also said that the wreckage appeared to have been on the beach for a long time, and suggested it probably came ashore sometime Monday. The unidentified floater spotted by the FRONTENAC's oiler would have been just offshore from the wreckage.

In the following days more wreckage reports reached the city. William Powell, a fisherman living at Powell's Point, near Munising, reported locating wreckage while running his fishing boat Monday along the east shore, below Pictured Rocks. Returning to Munising, Powell exhibited several selected pieces, including a built-in ladderway, stenciled in red "HENRY B. SMITH," an oar, also marked, two cabin doors, white outside and grained inside, two screens (red and green) for port and starboard running lights, two bed pillows, a green corduroy cushion and an armful of unused lifebelts. The wreckage was scattered as far east as Beaver Lake, 16 miles east of Munising. It all appeared to be from the upper works of the SMITH. Undoubtedly the steamer's superstructure had been torn to pieces, either while actually sinking or from the force of the gale. Additional wreckage was also located on Grand Island.

Periodic beach patrols continued to locate more wreckage east of Marquette, including many wooden hatch covers! Some of it, including glass fragments from the head lamps, stantions and a piece of door, was returned to Marquette and displayed at a local store.

In an effort to locate some of the missing bodies of the SMITH's crew, which had so far eluded the beach patrols, the Lake Carrier's Association requested that all State Game Wardens and deer hunters keep an eye open when near the shore. The search proved fruitless, and a rumor that two bodies had come ashore at Grand Marais was unsubstantiated. However, the steamer SAXONIA arrived in Portage Lake Sunday the 21st with the lifebelt-clad body of the SMITH's second cook. The SAXONIA had located it floating face down approximately 50 miles west of Whitefish Point.

It isn't difficult to visualize the SMITH's last few desperate hours. Shortly after departing Marquette, Captain Owen would have realized the error of leaving the safety of the harbor. The gale he thought was abating had grown in violence, and now held his ship firmly in its grasp.

Realizing that reaching the Soo under such conditions was impossible, he turned the ponderous steamer to port. Running directly into the seas, Owen tried to reach the shelter of Keweenaw Point. This was the turn the shore observers watched.

Heading directly into the gale punished the SMITH terrible. Mountainous seas crashed into her bow and battered the pilothouse. The same seas swept down the length of her open decks, tearing and grasping at each of her hastily-secured hatches. Finally, with sledge-hammer force they drove into the after cabin. Again and again the sequence was repeated! Again and again the SMITH shuddered from the repeated blows, but each time drove on. The tempest continued to grow.

Captain Owen fought the great storm with all the skill of his 30 years' experience, but he was slowly losing. Already several hatch covers had broken loose and great deluges of water flooded into the SMITH's hold with every wave.

Although the steam pumps ran constantly, they couldn't keep up with the flood. The monstrous greybeards slammed into her cabins, with devastating force, tearing away doors, ripping down wooden bulkheads and splintering furniture. The lifeboats had long since been torn off their davits. Their loss really made no difference. No small lifeboat could hope to live through that vortex of crashing water. The end for the SMITH and her 25-man crew was clearly at hand.

Ironically, one of the SMITH's crew did survive. He was the second mate John Burke, who left the ship in Marquette with a bad case of pneumonia. Interviewed later at his home, burke empathized with his lost comrades on the SMITH, stating "It's awful the way men struggle for life when death stares them in the face. God help those poor fellows. I know how it was with the wind and sleet blowing in their faces, beating the breath out of them for hours before the end came. The horror of shipwreck is in the waiting. Pray for sudden death and not that grinding warping twisting thing called drowning."

The SMITH had arrived in Marquette late Thursday night, November 6, after being delayed by gales. Friday morning she began to take on ore at the South Shore Dock, but the storm, which had delayed her arrival, continued to plague her, and the loading was far behind schedule. In the icy 24 degree weather, the ore frequently froze in the dock pockets and had to be knocked loose by hand. As soon as the loading was complete the steamer left the harbor before even battening her hatches. This was witnessed by the DENMARK and CHOCTAW crews.

Only two of the bodies of the 25 men on the SMITH were ever recovered. The first was that of the cook, found approximately two weeks after the wreck. The second was located in May of 1914 on Michipicoten Island by two Indians. Badly decomposed, it was identified as being that of the third engineer only by the papers in his pocket and an inscribed watch.

A possible explanation for the lack of additional bodies held that the wind and waves created such havoc along the south shore that the water line was abrubtly changed. Entire stretches of swamp and bayou were filled with sand, making them a solid mass of land. The SMITH's wreckage was discovered high up on the beach, indicating it came ashore at the height of the storm. Any bodies coming ashore at the same time would have been buried by the shifting sand, never to be discovered.

Speculation as to why Captain Owen took the SMITH out in dangerous conditions ran high. The Marquette Chronicle claimed the SMITH had been running late all season and that Owen was under pressure from the owners to "bring his ship home on time." It might have been this pressure that forced the captain to the foolhardiness of leaving port when he did.

After the story appeared, the Hawgood Company threatened a civil libel suit against the paper, claiming the story was false. Whether the action was ever pressed is unknown, but every vessel master was under pressure to make time. Ships don't earn money sitting at the dock. They make it in quick passages with many cargos.

Captain Owen commanded the SMITH since her maiden voyage in 1906, and was a veteran master for the Hawgoods. He had 30 years of Lake's experience, both in steam and sail,

and was considered to be an excellent mariner.

The question of why Owen left port can be answered simply. The storm lulled, and he thought the worst had passed. That his passage to the Soo would be rough was expected. Superior in November is never a docile lake. Owen also had enormous confidence in his vessel. He had been her master for seven years. She was staunch and seaworthy and should have been able to take a November gale in her stride.

How and why the SMITH sank is more difficult to answer. Most marine men felt that she lost her hatches and became waterlogged. While sinking, the waves swept her upper works clean, which accounted for the amount and type of wreckage located east of Marquette. The observation by the DENMARK and CHOCTAW crews concerning the unsecured hatches lends strength to this explanation.

Mr. J.R. Oldham, a well-known Cleveland marine architect of that era drew similar conclusions. He claimed that the hatch coamings were too low, being only 12 inches high when they should have been three feet, and that the hatch covers themselves should have been stronger and heavier. Oldham also said the steamers were underpowered, and were unable to make real headway in a wind. He further pointed out the importance of trimming and leveling off cargos of coal and ore, and claimed that several vessels were lost in the 1913 blow because their cargos shifted, throwing them on their beam ends. In that position water would pour through the hatches. This could have happened to the SMITH.

The hatches on the SMITH, as with all steamers of that period, were weak. The hatch covers were simply made of wood and covered by tarpaulins for water-tightness. During heavy weather the waves crashing on deck could force the wooden covers off. Subsequent waves would flood the cargo hold. Although the hatch covers were braced into position, too much reliance was placed on the actual weight of the cover to hold it in place on the hatch coaming.

There was some speculation that the large number of hatches (32) resulted in a structural weakness in the SMITH's upper deck. Under the tremendous strain of the gale, this weakness caused the steamer to break in two. There was little evidence, however, to support this theory.

The mystery of why the SMITH sank was further confused in June of 1914 when a message in a bottle was found by a fisherman at Mamaimse Point on the north shore, 35 miles from Whitefish Point. Dated November 12, the message as printed in the Marquette Mining Journal read: "Dear Sir: Steamer H.B. SMITH broke in two at the number five hatch. We are not able to save her. (line missing) Had one hard time on Superior. Went down 12 miles east of Marquette. Please give this to owners." The signature was not legible. The message was badly torn and faded, and was difficult to read.

After much consideration the owners concluded that the message was a fake. The major reason for this conclusion was the discrepancy in dates. The message was dated November 12, while the SMITH left Marquette on the 9th and probably sank that night or early on the 10th.

A possible clue to the reason for the SMITH's loss was uncovered in 1976 when four Wisconsin divers discovered the wreck of the 524-foot steamer ISSAC M. SCOTT, lost in

Lake Huron in the same gale that sank the SMITH. Located upside down in 175 feet of water, an examination of the wreck revealed the SCOTT's rudder was ripped loose from the bottom. With the rudder so damaged, she would have stood no chance in the storm. Could the rudder on the SMITH have received similar damage? Perhaps during her observed turn to port?

The approximate area of the SMITH's foundering could be presumed to be generally north and west of Marquette. This location would match up with the wreckage found on the shore east of Marquette, as a result of a northwest gale. Estimates of the distance from Marquette vary, ranging from 40 to 50 miles to as close as 15 to 20 miles. A lack of bodies would tend to indicate that the sinking was rapid and that the crew was trapped within. The finding of the cook's body wasn't considered significant, as local marine men felt the cooks were usually the first in the crew to don life belts. They suggested the cook was simply swept overboard, as was the engineer found on Michipicoten Island.

Some local marine men, however, thought the SMITH was more likely closer to Grand Island. Is the bottled message was authentic and the SMITH did sink 12 miles east of Marquette, the resulting wreckage would have probably washed ashore further east than where it was found.

The loss of the HENRY B. SMITH remains substantially unexplained, with only speculation to fill the void. The tragic fact remains that the HENRY B. SMITH, one of the staunchest steel vessels on the lakes turned up missing in the great gale of November 1913. As a point of macabre coincidence, Captain Owen had previously sailed on the steamer IOSCO, thereby seeing service on two of Superior's "went missing." The IOSCO, towing the schooner-barge OLIVE JEANNETTE, disappeared near the Huron Islands in 1905.

REFERENCES:
American Ship Building Company. **Profile and Decks of Hull 34-343**. September 25, 1905.
    Cabin Plan Hull 342-343. November 3, 1905.
Annual Reports of the Steamboat Inspection Service, Vol. 4. National Archives. Record Group 41.
Beeson's Marine Directory. 1913. pp. 161-174.
Daily Mining Gazette (Houghton). November 19, 25, 1913.
Daily Mining Journal (Marquette). November 9, 10, 11, 15-20, 22-25, 1913; June 4, 1914.
Evening News (Sault Ste. Marie). November 9, 13, 14, 22, 26, December 3, 1913.
Journal of the Life-Saving Station at Grand Marais. November 10-13, 1913. National Archives. Record Group 26.
Journal of the Life-Saving Station at Marquette. November 9-11, 1913. National Archives. Record Group 26.
Marquette Chronicle. June 4, 1914.
Wreck Report, Steamer Henry B. Smith. November 26, 1913. National Archives. Record Group 26.

VESSEL:	WYOMING
LOSS:	Storm Damage
DATE:	October 11, 1914
TYPE:	Steamer
LOCATION:	Off Au Sable Point

SYNOPSIS:
When caught in the throes of a wild lake storm, not all vessels came to an untimely end. Some survived, but only after suffering heavy damage. An example is the steamer WYOMING.

Bound up in ballast for Duluth, the WYOMING steamed into a strong northwester' when passing off Au Sable Point. In an attempt to turn and run before the storm for shelter, she fell off into the dangerous trough of the sea. Before she managed to claw her way back on course, she broke the main straps and fastenings to the hull and opened the topsides and deck amidships. In all the steamer received storm damages of $5,000, a considerable sum in 1914 for a vessel that never actually "wrecked."

REFERENCES:
Wells List. op. cit., p. 54.

VESSEL:	GALES STAPLES
LOSS:	Total
DATE:	October 1, 1918
TYPE:	Wooden Steamer
LOCATION:	Au Sable Reef

SYNOPSIS:
The 277-foot, 2,197-ton GALES STAPLES, loaded with coal, was upbound when a strong north gale blew her hard onto Au Sable Reef, about three quarters of a mile off shore and abreast of the Au Sable Point Lighthouse. The steamer was spotted by the Grand Marais Coast Guard Station Lookout at 4 p.m. Although the Keeper in charge of the station was absent on liberty, the Number One Surfman called all hands, and after launching the power surfboat, made their way out to the stranded steamer, reaching her about 5 p.m. The wreck was about eight miles to the west of the Station.

Since there was still hope of saving the steamer, the Coast Guard returned to Grand Marais without rescuing the crew, but instead with telegrams for the Soo calling for tugs and for the owners advising them of their vessel's plight. Later the Coast Guard returned to the steamer and stood by throughout the night.

At 8 a.m. on October 2, the Coast Guard returned from the GALES STAPLES bringing with them one seaman and two women cooks. They went back at 9:30 a.m. only to return again shortly after 2 p.m. with four seamen. When the Coast Guard crew returned to the steamer again at 5 p.m., the wind and seas had increased and seas were breaking aboard. Since there was danger of the ship breaking up, the Coast Guard took the captain and the ten remaining sailors off.

When the Grand Marais Coast Guard Station Keeper, Benjamin Truedell, arrived back at his post at 11 p.m. he

The 277 foot, 2,197 ton wooden steamer GALES STAPLES pictured while light (without cargo).   Dowling Collection

found a beehive of efficient activity. As normal, the early Coast Guardsmen were performing their difficult tasks like clockwork.

When the weather moderated on the 3rd, the Coast Guard, at the request of the STAPLE's captain, returned him and ten of his crew to the steamer. The captain was still optimistic about getting his charge off the reef. Keeper Truedell, however, had doubts. Wisely he cancelled any liberty for his crew and set them to preparing their equipment for further use. If a norther' blew up, as they were apt to at Au Sable, they would have to pluck the crew off quickly!

For the next three days the weather held and the Coast Guardsmen were employed in carrying telegrams out to the steamer advising her master of progress in sending the requested tugs.

On the 7th, the Great Lakes Towing Company tug ILLINOIS, with the lighter RELIANCE, arrived on the scene and the Coast Guard crew piloted them over the treacherous reef and alongside the STAPLES. The Coast Guard also transported A.C. Hansen, the Marine Insurance Agent, out to the wreck so he could personally assess the situation. After recovering about 1600 tons of the coal cargo, the salvors abandoned the steamer as hopeless, and a loss of $75,000.

The GALES STAPLES had earlier been the American steamer CALEDONIA. In 1917 she was sold Canadian and renamed.

REFERENCES:
Log of Coast Guard Station at Grand Marais, Michigan.
    October 1-8, 1918. National Archives, Record Group 26.

VESSEL:	WOOD ISLAND
LOSS:	Total
DATE:	September 9, 1922
TYPE:	Gas Tug
LOCATION:	Five Mile Point

SYNOPSIS:

One of the few fire losses in the Munising areas was that of the small 45-foot tug WOOD ISLAND on the night of September 9, 1922. The tug was enroute from Munising to the mouth of the Whitefish River with a string of 65 boom sticks when the accident happened. At 10 p.m. an engine on the tug backfired through the carbuetor, spraying burning gasoline throughout the interior of the cabin. It was thought that water in the gas caused the actual backfire. Although the Captain, Angus Steinoff and his two-man crew tried to extinguish the fire, they were not successful.

The crew stayed aboard until the flames threatened the rear gas tank, when they abandoned her in the yawl. Minutes later the tank exploded. A while later the forward tank blew with a roar and its flash illuminated the lake for hundreds of yards.

At 10:15 p.m. the WOOD ISLAND sank. Captain Steinoff estimated the wreck was about 1½ miles off Five Mile Point in approximately 60 feet of water.

The crew was rescued by the tug GRAND ISLAND, owned by the Cleveland Cliffs Iron Company (CCI). The WOOD ISLAND had planned to meet the GRAND ISLAND at 4 a.m. in Shelter Bay.

The small 45 foot gas tug WOOD ISLAND. Owned by the Cleveland Cliffs Iron Company she was used for towing log booms as well as transporting tourists and company personnel between Munising and Grand Island.

Marquette County Historical Society

It is interesting to note that such accidents today to gas powered boats are relatively uncommon as the result of Coast Guard regulations requiring the use of flame arrestors on carburetors.

The WOOD ISLAND was built by the Racine Boat Company in 1907 for Marcus A. Doty who used her in a passenger service between Munising, Grand Island and the Pictured Rocks. In 1917 she was purchased by CCI. When the tug joined the CCI fleet, she was modified, having a double tow post built in the stern and repowered with twin 40 horsepower Doman engines. CCI used her to tow log rafts from Grand Island to the company sawmill, as well as assist other company vessels in passenger service between Grand Island and Munising.

REFERENCES:
Daily Mining Journal (Marquette). September 12, 12, 1922.

VESSEL:	HERMAN H. HETTLER
LOSS:	Total
DATE:	November 23, 1926
TYPE:	Wooden Steamer
LOCATION:	Grand Island

SYNOPSIS:

The 210-foot, 789-ton wooden steamer HERMAN H. HETTLER was seeking shelter in Munising Harbor from a typical fall gale when a reported compass variation caused her to veer off course and slam into the rock reef off Trout Point, at the northeast end of the East Channel. The HETTLER, under Captain John M. Johnson, was enroute from Ludington, Michigan to Duluth with a cargo of 1,100

tons of bulk table salt. The accident happened about 8:30 p.m. and when visibility was restricted by heavy snow squalls.

The force of the grounding ran the steamer on the rocks up to her third hatch and forced her bow three feet out of the water! The seas were slamming into the HETTLER regularly, causing the steamer to "work" on the rocks, and slowly by steadily opening her seams. Blowing his whistle to attract attention, the captain kept his 16-man crew aboard and worked the pumps. The following day they launched their lifeboats and were towed by the fish tug PREBLE into Munising. From the town the Captain wired for assistance from the Great Lakes Towing Company and notified the vessel's owners.

Visiting the vessel on the 25th, the captain reported her at near total loss. She had pounded badly and opened many of her seams. The cargo hold was awash and the salt was rapidly dissolving! The next storm was expected to break the wreck completely.

Because of other demands for their services, and the relatively low value of the aged HETTLER, immediate assistance in the form of wrecking tugs was not forthcoming. This spelled the end for the HETTLER.

The much feared storm came on Friday the 26th. The northwester blew for 36 hours and finished off any chance for saving the HETTLER. During the storm, the stern of the steamer broke away and sank and her upperworks were completely swept away. When the results of the storm were assessed, she was officially abandoned and turned over to the underwriters.

The HETTLER, a 36-year veteran of the Lakes, was built in 1890 and rebuilt in 1913. Usually she worked in the lumber trade, although a brief foray off into bulk cargos like the salt

The wooden steamer HERMAN H. HETTLER, one of the wrecks that are strewn along Munising's West Channel.
Authors Collection

she carried on her last trip wasn't uncommon. Owned by the Wenonah Transportation Company of Michigan City, Michigan, she was a loss of $10,000. Insurance covered all of the cargo loss, but only $40,000 of the vessel's value.

Several years after the wreck, the hull, together with an old schooner near the Coast Guard station, was dynamited by the Coast Guard as a navigation hazard. Today nothing is left of the HETTLER other than broken hull timbers and miscellaneous pieces of minor structure and fittings. The water depth over the wreckage ranges from 10 to 40 feet.

The HETTLER had earlier been involved in another Lake Superior shipwreck incident. On November 5, 1925 she was downbound for Muskegon towing the 44-year-old, 187-foot barge JOHN L. CRANE. At the time, 10:30 p.m., a strong gale was howling but both vessels seemed to be making fair progress. Without warning the barge suddenly dove for the bottom and the tow post of the HETTLER tore out with a crash. Although the steamer did her best she wasn't able to rescue any of the barge's crew of six men and one woman. The loss occurred off Crisp Point.

REFERENCES:
Annual Report of the Lake Carrier's Association, 1925, p. 125; 1925, pp. 63-65.
Daily Mining Journal (Marquette). October 10, 1961.
Log of the U.S. Coast Guard Station at Grand Marais, November 24, 1926. National Archives. Record Group 26.
Munising News. November 26, December 23, 1926.
U.S. Coast Guard Report of Casualty, Steamer H.H. HETTLER. National Archives. Record Group 26.
Wells List. op. cit., p. 75.

VESSEL:	J.E. GORMAN
LOSS:	Recovered
DATE:	May 16, 1929
TYPE:	Steel Freighter
LOCATION:	Rock River (Au Train)

SYNOPSIS:

The 350-foot J.E. GORMAN was enroute from Buffalo to Houghton when a north gale accompanied by a blinding blizzard forced her to seek shelter in Grand Island Harbor. On the way in, she fell off course and lost her rudder when she touched bottom. Without her rudder, she drifted helplessly before the gale. To give her some control, the kedge anchor was dragged until the nearby shore was sighted through the snow squalls. Then both anchors were dropped. However, the force of the wind and sea were so strong she continued to drag her anchors until she grounded in Shelter Bay at 2 a.m. Until daybreak she blew continuous distress signals with her steam whistle and fired an occasional rocket. Since he had no radio aboard, the captain

The ice covered wreck of the steamer E.W. OGLEBAY on the beach off Marquette's Shot Point. The OGLEBAY was wrecked during a December 1927 blizzard and remained on the beach until May of 1929 when the Durocher Towing and Wrecking Company of De Tour hauled her free. Just days later, they also freed the steamer J.E. GORMAN.
Authors Collection

dropped an SOS message over the side in a buoy.

The stranded steamer was first sighted shortly after daylight by the crew of the South Shore train. The railroad men rapidly passed the word of the accident to the Coast Guard Station at Marquette.

When the Coast Guard arrived in their motor life boat they found the GORMAN hard aground but in no particular danger. A heavy northwest storm on the 18th caused the vessel to drag her anchors again and she slipped closer inshore. The GORMAN was now sitting firmly on a sand and rock bottom with her bow only several hundred feet off the beach.

The steamer was released on the 19th by the Durocher Towing and Wrecking Company of De Tour. Using the tug GENERAL and lighter DE TOUR, the GORMAN slipped off

surprisingly easily after lightering a mere 75 tons of coal and some fairly minor hull patching.

The Durocher wreckers had just finished releasing the steel freighter E.W. OGLEBAY from Marquette's Shot Point. The OGLEBAY had been on the beach for two years and her release was considered quite an accomplishment for the relatively unknown company.

The GORMAN had over $125,000 in damages. She had lost her rudder and shoe, had a hole in one of her tanks and numerous leaks in the stern. Owned by the Great Lakes Transit Company, the steamer was built in 1909.

REFERENCES:
Daily Mining Journal (Marquette). May 17, 20, 1929.
Wells List. op. cit., p. 78.

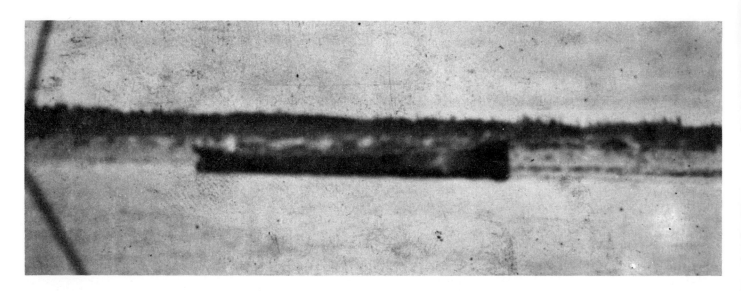

The LAKE FRUGALITY on the beach above Au Sable Point.   State Archives, Michigan Department of State

VESSEL:	LAKE FRUGALITY
LOSS:	Recovered
DATE:	October 22, 1929
TYPE:	Barge
LOCATION:	Au Sable Point

SYNOPSIS:

The 251-foot steel barge LAKE FRUGALITY was downbound from Marquette in the tow of the tug BARRALLTON when the tow cable parted in a northeast gale. The barge was blown on the beach about four miles west of Au Sable Point. The accident was caused by the failure of the tug's towing engine. The BARRALLTON sheltered safely behind Whitefish Point until the gale abated. The barge was salvaged with little effort by the BARRALLTON together with a Coast Guard vessel and a local fish tug.

REFERENCES:

Duluth News-Tribune. October 22-24, 1929. Michigan State Archives, Lansing, Michigan.

Wells List. op. cit., p. 79.

The 251 foot steel barge LAKE FRUGALITY.   Dowling Collection

Photograph on the left: A diver examines part of the KIOWA's shaft coupling. Note the large brass pillow block.
Photograph on the right: A diver emerges from a deck hatchway.

Authors Collection

VESSEL:	KIOWA
LOSS:	Total
DATE:	November 30, 1929
TYPE:	Steel Freighter
LOCATION:	Au Sable Reef

SYNOPSIS:

The KIOWA, a 251-foot, 2,309-ton steel steamer was downbound from Duluth to Chicago with a cargo of flax when she was overtaken by a fierce north storm accompanied by a freezing blizzard. In the midst of the blow, her cargo shifted, giving the steamer a heavy list. Helpless, the stricken KIOWA drifted before the seas.

Apparently, since the records are not clear, about fifteen miles northwest of Au Sable Light, while the sinking KIOWA was still drifting helplessly, her Captain Alex T. Young together with four of her crew abandoned the ship in her only lifeboat! The remaining sixteen of her crew were left aboard to shift for themselves.

From the KIOWA the remaining crew watched as the small lifeboat capsized. Of the original five occupants, only one was able to claw his way back in. The rest had apparently drowned. Meanwhile the KIOWA continued to drift down the Michigan coast. The Mate, Arthur Kronk, left in charge by the "abdication" of the captain, tried to keep order among the near panicked crew. With death staring them all bang in the eye, it wasn't easy.

The next day, December 1, at 3:15 p.m., the Coast Guard crew at Grand Marais was busy repairing their submarine telephone cable when they heard the Au Sable Point fog signal blowing several long and short blasts, a pre-arranged call of distress.

Dropping the repair job, the Coast Guard crew manned the power lifeboat and headed for the light station. The blizzard had left deep snow drifts, ruling out any attempt at moving overland. The lake, although storm tossed and frigid, was still the best highway available. At 4:30 p.m. they arrived at the light and learned from the keeper that the KIOWA, of Michigan City, had fetched up on the reef.

It isn't clear exactly who rescued the sixteen survivors of the KIOWA, or from where! One source states it was the boat from the light house together with a hunter's boat. The hunters were marooned at the light by the storm. Apparently the light keeper ordered them out after the Coast Guard failed to arrive in what he considered adequate time.

Another source claims the rescue was made by two local fishermen, Richard Chilson and his son Charles. They reportedly were waiting out the storm with their small gas powered tug pulled safely up on the beach at the Hurricane River when they sighted the KIOWA in distress. In both of the above stories, the survivors were brought to safety at the Lighthouse.

The official Coast Guard Log is crystal clear in all aspects of the KIOWA disaster except that concerning exactly how the survivors were actually rescued from the ship. The Log gives the impression that the Coast Guard crew, after arriving at the lighthouse and learning of the wreck, then proceeded to the KIOWA and rescued the sixteen crewmen. The official telegram (number 9902) to the Commander of the Eleventh Coast Guard District notifying him of the wreck, gave the Coast Guard crew the credit, stating, "picked off 16 men from steamer KIOWA, five lost, one body recovered." Whether the ambiguity was intentional to cover the embarrassment of the Coast Guard in "missing" a major rescue is debatable. Regardless, the Coast Guard crew returned to the Grand Marais Station with the survivors at 7:30 p.m. Since local hotel space could not be found, the bedraggled survivors were quartered at the Coast Guard Station.

The KIOWA's drifting lifeboat was discovered about 2 p.m. by the Grand Marais tug JOSEPHINE ADDISON. In it was the frozen body of one of the crew. Although the man regained the lifeboat after it capsized, he couldn't protect himself from the terrible cold. As a result of hypothermia, he froze to death.

There was no immediate respite for the Coast Guard crew. At midnight on December 2, the Station Watchman sighted a steamer off the harbor entrance making distress signals. Immediately the Station fired a Costin signal in return, and launched the power lifeboat. Reaching the steamer, which turned out to be the GEORGE H. DONOVAN, the crew was requested to pilot her into the harbor for shelter. The crew completed the task with dispatch.

At 6 p.m., the Alger County Coroner, a Dr. Scholtes, arrived at the Station from Munising, rapidly impaneled a jury and held an inquest for the recovered body. Subsequently it was identified as that of Mike Westenberg, one of the KIOWA's crew. The good doctor also gave the survivors a quick physical and determined that two required hospitalization and should return with him to the Munising Hospital.

On Tuesday the 3rd, the Coast Guard crew took the power lifeboat with the smaller surfboat in tow and returned to Au Sable Light. Since the lake was still rolling, they anchored the lifeboat about a quarter mile out and used the oar powered surfboat to run the breakers and make a safe landing on the sandy beach. There they took aboard four marooned hunters and one more of the KIOWA's crew, either lost in the shuffle during the original rescue or purposefully left behind due to overcrowding. The trip back through the breakers in the small surfboat was very difficult since the boat and oars had badly iced up in the freezing

weather. They all arrived safe back at the Grand Marais Station but did have to break ice all the way from the harbor entrance to the Coast Guard dock.

Heavy weather prevented the KIOWA's underwriters from getting out to their vessel until December 7. Then a lull allowed the Coast guard to ferry them out to the KIOWA. Earlier, on the 5th, an attempt using the tug ADDISON was made but she was driven back by a strong northwest sea. After the vessel and her cargo were examined for over an hour both the underwriters and hull inspectors felt both were a total loss.

For several years following the wreck, the Whitefish population in the Grand Marais area apparently increased dramatically, since the fish thrived on the flax seed oils and proteins. Local fishermen shipped large quantities down to Chicago markets, which was just as well since the fish reportedly tasted strongly of linseed oil!

During World War II, much of the steel superstructure and part of the hull was salvaged for scrap. However, a great amount of the vessel still remains.

The KIOWA had an earlier scrape on Lake Superior. On July 24, 1928 she stranded in fog on Parisienne Island at the foot of Whitefish Bay.

Her Mate Arthur Kronk's involvement in Lake Superior shipwreck wasn't over. On May 27, 1933, he was the mate of the 259-foot passenger steamer GEORGE M. COX when she plowed into Rock of Ages Reef in a fog. Mate Kronk held the watch when she hit and was subsequently blamed during the investigation for not keeping the proper course.

The KIOWA was the result of an emergency shipbuilding program started during World War I. Under the program a total of 331 similar vessels were eventually built. Although the program continued for a time after the war ended, in 1920 it was cancelled, leaving many shipyards with still unfinished vessels on the ways. With private financing twenty of these vessels were finished in the hope of selling them at a profit. The KIOWA was one of the twenty. Built in 1920 by the Detroit Ship Building Company, she measured 251 feet by 43 feet by 24 feet.

REFERENCES:

Annual Report of the Lake Carriers Association, 1930. p. 54.

Dowling, Reverend Edward J. **Know Your Lakers of World War I**. Sault Ste. Marie, Michigan: Marine Publishing Company, 1978, pp. 43, 91-93.

Letter, Axel Neimi, to author, March 15, 1977.

Log of Au Sable Light Station. December 1, 1929. National Archives, Record Group 26.

Log of the Grand Marais Coast Guard Station. December 1-7, 1929. National Archives, Record Group 26.

Wells List. op. cit., p. 80.

Wreck Report, Steamer KIOWA, December 1, 1929. National Archives, Record Group 26.

The 247 foot Canadian steamer GEORGIAN photographed during the opening of the new Welland Canal.

Dowling Collection

VESSEL:	GEORGIAN
LOSS:	Recovered
DATE:	November 28, 1932
TYPE:	Freighter
LOCATION:	Grand Island, Trout Point

SYNOPSIS:

The 247-foot, 2,484-ton Canadian steamer GEORGIAN ran aground on a rock reef off Trout Point while trying to find shelter from a heavy lake storm. She was freed the following May.

REFERENCES:
Duluth News-Tribune. November 30, 1932.

The SPARTA in Munising Harbor just after being released by Merritt Chapman and Scott. The tug alongside is the

WILLIAM A. WHITNEY.
Hamilton Collection

VESSEL:	SPARTA
LOSS:	Recovered
DATE:	November 5, 1940
TYPE:	Steel Steamer
LOCATION:	Pictured Rocks

SYNOPSIS:

The last of the major Pictured Rocks shipwrecks was that of the 4,307-ton SPARTA during the night of November 5, 1940. The 380-foot steamer was east of Grand Island when the powerful winds of a vicious north gale blew her aground at the west end of Mosquito Beach, about fourteen miles east of Munising. Since the ship was in no immediate danger of sinking, the crew wisely stayed aboard until the gale diminished.

At 7:15 a.m. on November 7, Coast Guardsman Eugene Pasguinelli of the Munising (Sand Point) Station sighted a lifeboat coming around Castle Rock. Even though the occupants were rowing, it had a small sail up and to the Coast Guardsman's trained eye, she looked like she was in trouble. Within one half hour the Coast Guardsmen had launched their surfboat and were alongside the strange lifeboat. Bobbing about in the middle of Munising Bay they learned of the wreck of the SPARTA.

After bringing the lifeboat's sixteen man crew to the station, the Coast Guardsmen launched the motor lifeboat and headed for the wreck, arriving alongside her at 10 a.m., after a run of an hour and fifteen minutes. At the SPARTA they rescued 21 additional members of the crew.

At 1 p.m. the Coast Guard crew returned to the SPARTA with the ship's officers and officials of the U.S. Steamboat Inspection Service to allow them to make a detailed examination to assess the charges of salvage. In case they were needed, the Coast Guard Cutters RUSH and OSSIPPI

were also standing by.

During the next five days the Munising crew was constantly relaying messages between the wrecking crew on the SPARTA and the shore, as well as transporting various personnel. On November 10, the Coast Guard crew received word that the SPARTA would be abandoned as a total loss. The famous wrecking tug FAVORITE had also tried to free the steamer, but failed.

In spite of the decision to abandon the SPARTA, there would be little rest for the Munising crew. On the night of November 12, they received a message from the Michigan Conservation Department that the steamer SINALOA was in trouble near Fayette on northern Lake Michigan. Loading up their gear in the station truck, they left to perform another rescue!

The SPARTA was finally recovered in June of 1941 by the wrecking firm of Merritt, Chapman and Scott of Duluth, but never sailed again. The salvors discovered her back was broken. She would end up spending the rest of her days as a dock for the Roen Towing Company of Sturgeon Bay, Wisconsin. Originally the SPARTA had been built as the Gilchrist freighter FRANK W. HART, thus making her another former Gilchrist vessel eventually lost!

REFERENCES:
Duluth News-Tribune. November 9-10, 1940.
Log of the Munising Coast Guard Station, November 5-15, 1940. National Archives, Record Group 26.
Log of the Grand Marais Coast Guard Station, November 7, 1940. National Archives, Record Group 26.
Van de Linden, Rev. Peter J., ed. **Great Lakes Ships We Remember**. Cleveland: Freshwater Press, 1979. p. 365.

SPARTA on the beach.

A view of the SPARTA on the beach. Take note of how far out the vessel is forward. The small boat alongside is a 36 foot Coast Guard motor lifeboat.

Hamilton Collection
Rutherford B. Hayes Library

VESSEL:	ROAMER
LOSS:	Total
DATE:	July 3, 1949
TYPE:	Trolling Boat
LOCATION:	West Channel

SYNOPSIS:

The waters around Grand Island and the Pictured Rocks coast have always been prone to quick and dangerous changes of weather. In many instances both large commercial vessels and small craft were caught unaware by violent squalls welling up over the hills to the south of Munising. The sinking of the ROAMER is a good example of the sudden danger that can cause the rapid loss of both vessel and life.

On Sunday, July 3, 1949, the 30 foot trolling boat ROAMER with nine men aboard was fishing in an area northwest of Grand Island when disaster struck. Although the weather was clear and calm, without warning, what appeared to be a strong squall boiled over the hills surrounding the town. Spotting the ugly black clouds to the south, hearing the loud thunder and knowing the evil weather promised, the ROAMER headed for safety in Munising Bay.

About 4 p.m., when the ROAMER had reached the outer reaches of the West Channel between Wood Island and Grand Island, the storm struck with terrific fury. It's intensity was so great that some reported it to have been nothing less than a tornado! The once calm lake was whipped into a maelstrom of wave and wind and lashed by buckets of storm driven rain.

The men aboard, seeing the approach of the storm, had donned life-jackets, prepared for the worst. It was a wise precaution. The storm made short work of the ROAMER, swamping her quickly. The boat was nearly sunk, only two feet of her bow left bobbing above the water. Nearby the men drifted in the midst of the waves. Some were supported only by their life-jackets while others clung to part of the boats wooden roof, ripped off in the storms first onslaught. Although it was July, the water was numbing cold. If rescue didn't come soon, there would be no reason for it to come at all. All would be dead!

In an hour the terrible storm calmed a bit. The winds were just a little less screaming and the waves a little less tremendous.

Something more than two hours after the ROAMER swamped the numbed survivors saw a truly magnificent sight, that of a fast cruiser heading out from Munising and knifing her way through the crashing seas directly for them. Time after time, the tumbling waves threatened to swamp the boat as they did the ROAMER, but each time

skillful handling brought the strange vessel through unscathed.

The boat was piloted by Captain Everett Morrison. Also aboard was Bert Lehman. Normally Morrison used the boat to take tourists on excursions past the Pictured Rocks. But today he was heading out to rescue a friend. Captain Lukowski of the ROAMER was his friend and neighbor and they had made a pact that if disaster struck and one didn't come in from the lake, the other would go out and search. Captain Morrison rescued eight men from ROAMER, but the ninth, Captain Lukowski, was dead, having suffered what was thought to have been a fatal heart attack when his vessel swamped.

When Morrison returned to the city dock with the bedraggled survivors, the shore was lined with several hundred spectators all waiting anxiously to see if the search had been successful.

All of the men recovered from their experience, but were it not for the heroics of Captain Everett Morrison and Bert Lehman, all would surely have perished.

REFERENCES:
East, Ben. **Narrow Escapes and Wilderness Adventures.** New York: E.P. Dutton & Co. 1960.
Marquette Mining Journal. July 5, 6, 1949.

ADDITIONAL ACCIDENTS

1828   OTTER, sail vessel, owned by the North-West Fur Company, built in 1813 and lost with all hands in a gale off Grand Sable Banks.

1858   AMERICAN REPUBLIC, bark, disabled in a storm, reaching Grand Island with $700 in damages.

1870   G.W. SCOTT, schooner, stranded on Grand Island with little damage.

1870   GEORGE W. HOLT, schooner, ashore in a gale at Grand Island with $800 in damages.

1873   PELICAN, schooner, ashore at Sand Point with little damage.

1879   ANNIE COLEMAN, schooner, driven ashore by a storm near the Hurricane River, crew hiked to Marquette to report disaster. Vessel was a total loss.

1882   GENERAL SIGEL, schooner, ashore at Au Sable Point with $1,000 in damages.

1882   ECLIPSE, schooner, ashore at Au Sable Point with $800 in damages.

1882   SOUTHWEST, schooner, sunk near Grand Island with $3,500 in damages. She was later recovered.

1883   GEORGE SHERMAN, schooner, stranded at Grand Island with minor damages. In 1887 the SHERMAN would be involved in a major shipwreck at Shot Point, several miles east of Marquette.

1884   MYSTIC, schooner, stranded on Au Sable Point with slight damages.

1894   Fish boat (no name), wrecked with the loss of two lives near Powell Point.

1896   VOLUNTEER, schooner, ashore four miles west of Au Sable Point.

1898   ESCANABA, steamer ashore near Grand Island but released after jettisoning a portion of her cargo of salt.

1908   L.H.E., small sailboat, discovered blown ashore near Au Sable Point. The lone occupant, a crewman from the Grand Island Light Station, was found dead from exposure.

1910   CATIGEE, wooden steamer, survived a northwest blow only by jettisoning 40 horses from her cargo to lighten ship.

1913   CARLOTTA, gas screw, lost off Grand Island as the result of a fire. No lives were lost.

1913   VAN ALLEN, steamer, when off Grand Island lost deck cargo of 60 bales of hay during heavy weather. The storm also required several days of vessel repair in Munising harbor.

1914   EDWARD MC WILLIAMS, barge, lost in a gale by the steamer GREEN off the Pictured Rocks. Luckily the barge's anchors caught before she was blown directly into the Grand Portal and destroyed.

1923   ROTARIAN, 147 foot, 307 ton wooden excursion steamer that suffered extensive ($15,000) engine damages while near Grand Island.

1929   ALICE L. Fish tug, lost east of Au Sable Point with the loss of one life.

1943   MARYMAID, a small fishing craft lost off Munising.

1959   Fish boat (no name), a small 20 foot fishing craft lost in the West Channel during a north squall drowning three fishermen.

1973   Fishing boat, lost off Five Mile Point when swamped by heavy seas. There was no loss of life.

The 730 foot, 21,500-ton ALGOBAY at safe anchor in Munising Bay thanks to the efforts of local commercial fishermen.

ADDENDUM

SUPERIOR (page 12)

One of the SUPERIOR's two unique triple tubed boilers. They are the only visible remnants of her power plant.

Authors Collection

Part of the SUPERIOR's hull and ribs. Usually covered by shifting bottom sands, the ribs were last exposed in 1981.

Authors Collection

THE ALGER GREAT LAKES BOTTOMLAND PRESERVE, A VIEWPOINT

In July of 1980, the Michigan Legislature passed and Governor William Milliken signed Public Act 184, the Underwater Preserve Act of 1980. This new law in part directs the state to "..... protect and preserve, and to regulate the taking of aboriginal records and antiquities within this state; to preserve abandoned property of historic or recreational value on the bottomlands of the Great Lakes and regulate the salvage of abandoned property of historical or recreational value; to designate Great Lakes bottomland preserves; and to prescribe penalties."

Thanks to the Michigan Department of Natural Resources rapid action was taken and at least some of the Great Lakes historic and recreationally valuable wrecks will be preserved for the future.

The Underwater Salvage Committee of the Michigan Department of Natural Resources (DNR) recommended several areas to be designated as Great Lakes bottomlands preserves under P. A. 184 to the states' Natural Resources Commission. One area designated was in Alger County, near the town of Munising. The area is now officially known as the Alger Great Lakes Bottomland Preserve. A second preserve was also designated in the Thunder Bay area, near Alpena.

A unique aspect of the designation procedure was that much of the vital groundwork for the selection of the Alger area as an underwater preserve was accomplished by a volunteer citizens committee.

The committee members included representatives of the Chamber of Commerce, dive charter operators, dive shop owners, local divers, area dive instructors, Alger County Historical Society, Pictured Rocks National Lakeshore, Michigan State University Extension Service, interested citizens and Michigan Sea Grant.

The committee evaluated the area closely, considering: (1) variety and number of material and/or cultural features, (2) historical significance, (3) recreational significance, (4) diving feasibility and quality, (5) public support, (6) economic impact, (7) management potential, (8) threatened resources, (9) proximity to major urban areas, (10) complementary onshore recreational facilities, (11) amount known about underwater resources. These were the same criteria the Natural Resources Commission would eventually use.

The committee, known as the Alger Underwater Preserve Committee, is still in place and functioning as an unofficial coordinating group. Recent accomplishments include establishing a diver emergency evacuation plan, selecting an Alger Preserve logo, and producing promo-tional brochures. In addition, it continues to serve as a vital unofficial coordinating committee for preserve operations. Future projects under consideration include bouying wrecks and locating additional preserve resources (shipwrecks-dive sites).

In addition to the wreck sites, the Munising area also offers numerous unique underwater geological formations such as caves, indents and spectacular colorful rock formations. Many of these sites and some of the shallow wrecks are well suited for exploration by snorkelers. Notable among the snorkel sites are the old docks which abound with artifacts from the heyday of lumbering as well as the ghostly remains of old fish tugs.

All of the sites are accessible to divers, either through one of the licensed charter boats operators, or by private boats launched from the municipal marina.

The popularity of the Alger preserve continues to increase; in 1970 an estimated 140 divers explored the wrecks. In 1980 the number rose to 1,540, a better than tenfold increase! The diver count for 1981 reached 2,800 and for 1982, an incredible 4,000! The 1980 - 82 figures are produced through the efforts of the Alger Underwater Preserve Committee and are accurate to plus/minus 5%.

The great potential of the preserve can be best understood when it is realized that of an estimated three million sport divers in the United States, 750,000 live in the midwest (Great Lakes) region and that Munising is within a days drive for all of them. In an age of galloping inflation and the importance of stretching the diving dollar, the relative closeness of such an exciting diving area achieves a growing importance.

The historical importance of the shipwrecks and the underwater geology of the area, make the underwater preserve an excellent arena for teaching. The preserve can be an important outdoor laboratory for the study of coastal geology, ecology and history.

The preserve also offers the potential of multiple recreational use for different groups, to include not only divers and snorkelers, but also boaters, fishermen, photographers, and historians. With the possible eventual development of a visitor interpretive center, the underwater preserve can serve an even larger segment of the public.

In establishing the underwater preserve, the State of Michigan has taken the first step. Now it's up to the Great Lakes diver to make it work so that future generations of divers can explore the unique underwater geological formations of Lake Superior as well as experience the awe and majesty of diving her shipwrecks.

ABOUT THE AUTHOR

Frederick Stonehouse holds a Master of Arts degree in American History from Northern Michigan University and has also authored four books on Lake Superior vessel losses: **Isle Royale Shipwrecks, Went Missing II, the Wreck of the Edmund Fitzgerald** and the most recent, **Lake Superior's "Shipwreck Coast"**. Stonehouse has lectured throughout the Midwest on diving and shipwreck exploration in the Great Lakes. His articles have appeared in **Skin Diver Magazine, Diver, International Diver's Guide** and **Nor' Easter** magazines. He has directed special shipwreck sureys for the Parks Canada and for Northern Michigan University and is an active consultant in Great Lakes history for various private and government agencies. He is a member of the Great Lakes Historical, Detroit Marine Historical and the Alger, Delta and Marquette County Historical Societies, the Great Lakes Maritime Institute, the Lake Superior Marine Museum Association and a member of the Board of Directors of the Marquette Maritime Museum Association. He is also a licensed Coast Guard master for all of the Great Lakes and a partner in Sonar Search Associates, a firm specializing in searching for new shipwrecks. Stonehouse is a Captain, Corps of Engineers, Michigan Army National Guard and makes his home in Marquette, Michigan.